ZERO EMI

Unlock Your Financial Freedom

"A useful book to help one become debt free and attain financial freedom"

Dr. Soma Valliappan
Writer, Expert in Finance

Ra Ma. Palaniappan

INDIA · SINGAPORE · MALAYSIA

Notion Press

No. 8, 3rd Cross Street,
CIT Colony, Mylapore,
Chennai, Tamil Nadu – 600 004

First Published by Notion Press 2020
Copyright © Ra Ma. Palaniappan 2020
All Rights Reserved.

ISBN 978-1-64899-947-5

Contents

Foreword

I find the book with lots of useful information, strong logic, and practical solutions. It is an easy to read book written with genuine concern for others. I am sure that the readers will be convinced of what you suggest and will become Debt free and attain financial freedom.

I wish you all the best!

Dr. Soma Valliappan
Writer, Trainer & Management Consultant.
Author of Bestselling Personal Finance Books such as
Alla Alla Panam and Bulls & Bears: All about Shares

–I–

Introduction

There are hundreds of books teaching you how to attain "financial freedom", talking about multiplying money, retiring early, building a retirement corpus, becoming rich and what not. All existing hacks become useless when your wallet has a hole. You earn hard with the hope to save, invest, and become wealthy. But even before you could save, your monthly bills and EMIs are to be paid off. Imagine what you save after paying all your bills. Financial Freedom is about living comfortably and having choices. But, what choices can you make when you are living under a debt mountain and savings is completely out of sight?

Savings is not an expense; it is an investment – well, sounds easy! So, where is the money to save when your income is not even enough to pay your bills off and you are short of money all the time? You only earn to cater to your EMIs, not to attain your financial goals. The debts that surround, stop you from reaching your goals quicker. Forget about reaching them faster, the majority of the time people do not reach their goals at all because of the debts they have, EMIs they must honor. Debts are real leakages that stop you from attaining financial freedom.

My childhood friend Ajay works for a shipping agency. He always grumbles about his job. His daily routine is somewhat: He must go to the harbor, work on the freight inward, later outward, almost be at the harbor the entire day, and then must return to the office in the evening for preparing reports. Toward the end of the month, he has additional work as his usual routine. He must prepare MIS and reconcile the monthly transactions. Ajay hates his job. He always says, "What job is this? I don't know what I'm doing. It isn't even relevant to what I studied. This isn't something that I've wanted to do. I feel like leaving this job," *bla, bla, bla.* With all these complaints, you know what? He still goes to that job. And, do you know why? Commitment, not the commitment toward his job, but the commitment toward EMIs.

Many are like my friend Ajay, tied to EMIs, loans and mortgages, and do not have control of money. In fact, it is the money that controls most of the time. You are stuck because of your financial commitments. At the same time, quite naturally, you are longing for financial freedom. How is it possible to reach place *a* by driving toward place *b*? It is not logical, is it? Dreams are good, but really essential to have a plan to achieve your dreams. Clearing your debts and abstaining from them is the first step to financial freedom, else all your efforts to attain financial freedom is not going to work. Once you stop leakages, that is when hacks in the way to get richer will start working. You must have "Zero EMI" to reach your financial goals and start living your dream life.

This book gives a blueprint for a "Zero EMI life". This book will help you understand how you can control your finances instead of being controlled by them. You will learn to stop the leakages— your debts, EMIs—and take the next steps toward financial freedom. This book was written out of my life experiences and personal stories about how I came out of debts and attained my financial goals. Good luck.

–II–

Why Do I Cry About Debts?

I had a terrible childhood that I wanted to forget.

I was in eighth grade, when we were living in an apartment wherein I had many friends. We played together and had lots of fun. I was the cricket team captain. The properties of the team: the bat, ball, stumps, everything would be in my home under my custody. No one could touch them without my permission. If they touched, I would fight, I would shout and ensure that they did not dare touch them again. I felt like a king until my father quitted his job.

My father left his job and started a printing business. He did not have the business acumen, due to which he faced a lot of hardships to develop the business. The income from the business was only enough to pay the rent, salary, electricity, and other essentials. To run the family and the business, my father started taking loans. Within a year, my family landed in a huge financial crisis. Debts piled up. Taking one loan to repay another or closing one loan and starting a new loan became a routine. We had unsolicited visitors, every day to our home, asking for their dues.

Everything around me started changing—my school, my books, my friends, my house. Everything. One thing that remained constant was debt. An old proverb says, 'Better go to bed hungry than wake up in debt.' Unfortunately, I experienced both.

We moved to a new house as we could not afford the rent of the current one. I did not get any friends around my new house. I got into a new school, where I did not like going as I was still attached to my old school. What had hurt me the most was giving back the cricket team's properties. I wept and cried as if the whole world was gone. No one was able to console me. The king in me was broken.

The entire family spent sleepless nights. I grew up; after graduating from college, I took up multiple employments. 10 years later, we were able to pay off our debts. What a relief it was? No more visitors asking for money, no more phone calls asking for dues. A breeze I enjoyed thoroughly. After being debt-free, I started feeling like a king again. However, I spent the prime time of my life thinking about the debt. Those 10 years was a tough time. I was always occupied with the thoughts about the loans to be repaid. Moreover, it was about coming out of debt as soon as possible. I never had a chance to think about my future, my career plan, my goals. The only financial goal I had was to clear off my debts. Could I call it a financial goal? I was just working to repay my debts, my bills and not toward anything else.

It is true that humans long for what they do not have. I have always longed for a debt-free life.

Having cleared off the debts, I started from scratch. It is natural for human beings to compare. When I compare myself with my friends, I lag behind my friends by almost 10 years. I have spent a decade working to repay my loans.

Only after those tough 10 long years, I was able to dream of financial freedom; I was able to determine my financial goals. I started saving money for my own house, for my own car, for my retirement corpus, etc. By that time, my friends had already settled, along with having kids.

Since then, I have been practicing debt-free life and advocate the same to others. I think it makes sense for me to do so. I do not want you to make a bad decision and end up in loans. I do not want you to suffer and stress over repaying your loans. I do not want you to spend the prime time of your career and your life, working to repay loans. I do not want you to get into a debt trap and give your children a pathetic childhood and your family a miserable life.

Imagine these adverse situations; your child needs an extra notebook and you are not able to buy it. Your wife is badly in need of a new stove for she was struggling with a troublesome one for years together and you are not able to buy it. You need an extra set of dress for office wear and you are not able to buy it. It is too much stress when you have a compelling expense and do not have money to meet it. It only leads you to stress. For bigger expenses, the only choice you have is to take a loan.

I have walked the path that was full of debts and can tell you how horrible it was. I do not want you to take that route, undergo the sufferings and then start from scratch. I want you to enjoy financial freedom, possess the ability to make choices at your will and live a stress-free life, financially.

One day, my daughter brought a circular home. It read that the football coaching classes at her school would commence from the next month. At that time, we were looking for a good football coaching center to enroll our daughter, as she loved to play football. There was none in our neighborhood. The hunt was on. The circular came in the meantime. What could be a better place than her own school to join for football coaching? However, the catch was to pay the fee immediately, which was ₹4,000. It was the 28th of that month and most of the salaried people would not have the luxury of spending in thousands during the month-end, for items like this. In case, there was no money in hand, there were only two choices: 1) Borrow money from someone; 2) Let the kid forego the coaching class.

In my case, I do not have any EMIs to pay. I enjoy financial freedom to make my own choices comfortably. I immediately paid the money without waiting for the next pay cheque and enrolled my kid for the football coaching class. Needless to say, my daughter was so happy and that happiness as a child was priceless. I am so happy that I was able to give that happiness to her.

Many people say, to attain financial freedom, you must have lots of wealth. Right? In my view, to attain financial freedom, you must get rid of your debt as when there is a hole, how much ever you pour, it is going to leak. You might never be able to fill back again. You must first stop the leakage. Debt is a leakage; you must cover that up first to grow wealth and attain financial freedom.

–III–

Debt is Dangerous

Debt is a leakage and that is why I think it is dangerous to keep. Before saying why debt is dangerous, let me tell you what debt really is. If you spend the money not yet earned, then it is a debt. You borrow money thinking that your future income will cover this. What if there is no *income* in the future? In such cases, which is in majority, the future of a few families goes for a toss.

We keep hearing stories of organizations letting go of their employees, factories shutting down, manufacturers reducing the paid hours. All these results in either job loss or reduced income. When I spoke to many such employees, they were found in a terrific state of mind. They are scared about their future, having huge EMIs in front of them. Absolutely, no clues about how to manage loans. They were cursing the organization, the management for their pathetic situation. Many fear job losses because of the huge EMIs to pay. This gives us a lot of insecurity, leading to a stressful life. To stick to the job, you make a lot of adjustments in terms of living up with a tough boss, poor job role, work overload and what not. If you do not have an EMI to be paid, if you do not have loans, do you think you fear job loss? Nope. That is exactly why I say: 'Debt is dangerous.' By the way, my idea is not to scare you. The whole idea is to get a better understanding of debt, stop drowning in it, learn to be financially free and make choices at will.

When I was watching television, I saw a news about a family committing suicide. What I learned that day was even more shocking. The family committed suicide because they could not repay their loans and withstand the debt collector's approaches and follow-ups. If that family did not have any loans, if they did not have anything to repay, would you think they could have committed suicide? Nope. That is exactly why I say that 'Debt is dangerous.' By the way, my idea is not to scare you. The whole idea is to get a better understanding of debt, stop drowning in it, learn to be financially free and make choices at will.

My uncle used his credit card extensively for shopping, beyond his means. When the credit card statement came, he did not worry much. He paid the minimum amount due and continued shopping. Every month the statement would come, my uncle will pay the minimum amount due and continue to shop. Over a period, he ended up paying double the amount of what he spent. There was a late fee, with interest on the outstanding amount and other penalties. When it comes to loans, the most crucial component is "interest". Friends, like people in IT, interest also does not sleep. There is no holiday period for loans. *Assets take holidays, but loans do not. If my uncle avoided using the credit card, if he had paid the full amount rather than the minimum amount due, do you think he'd have ended up paying double the amount?* No. That is exactly why I say,

'Debt is dangerous.' By the way, my idea is not to scare you. The whole idea is to get a better understanding of debt, stop drowning in it, learn to be financially free and make choices at will.

Now, you would have got a better idea of why debt is dangerous. So, stay away from debt. People argue that debt is essential for the economy to grow and I am misleading them by saying not to borrow money. If no one borrows money, how will the economy grow? In my view, the debt or EMIs are not the fuel for the economy, but consumption is. Consumption keeps the money moving from one place to another. If there is no consumption, then the growth stagnates. The problem is: when consumption uses debt—borrowed money. Debt-driven economy keeps the bankers, credit card companies, lawyers, judicial systems busy. It keeps them in business. The common, salaried people are the victims in the name of offers and EMIs. I do not say no to consumption but to EMIs. Spend your money—the money earned. That will be the real boom for you and also the economy.

–IV–

Good Debt Vs Bad Debt

You may be thinking of buying a house and its value is huge and cannot be paid from savings. Should *you* take a loan? The previous chapter said that debt is dangerous. Friends, the most important consideration while taking a loan is whether the debt incurred is good debt or bad debt.

Good Debt

If you are taking a loan for an item that would grow in value, then it is good debt. For example: housing loan, business loan and educational loan. Let me explain to you why these are good debts.

Housing Loan: You need lakhs and lakhs of rupees to buy a house. Many may not be able to buy houses from the cash in their hand. The natural choice is to take a bank loan. The bank would charge interest for the loan. The total cost of a house is the loan amount plus the interest payable. The value of the house would grow or appreciate over a period and should be able to surpass the total cost of the house. So, it is advisable to take loans for buying a new house.

Business Loan: You need money to start a business. The businesses run with an objective to make a profit, i.e., making more money than invested. The interest charged by the bank can be paid out of the profit that the business makes. In the case of business loans, the value of the money grows.

Educational Loan: Spending toward education is not an expense, it is an investment. It would educate the child, expand the mind so that they take the right steps toward life and career. Educational loans are mostly taken for high-value professional courses, for which the returns are equally lucrative. The child gets an employment opportunity with the education gained and that employment pays him or her for a lifetime. Education uplifts not only the individual, but also the entire family and the generations to follow.

For example, I took an education loan for ₹63,000 to get an MBA course at ICFAI University. I completed an MBA in International Business, which gave me a competitive edge during the job search. I got placed with Standard Chartered Bank. It opened the door of opportunities and my steady income. In my opinion, education is good debt.

Bad Debt

If you take a loan for an item that would grow in value, then it is good debt, whereas for items that would decline in value, it is bad debt. For example: home appliances, mobile phones and cars. Let me explain to you why these are bad debts.

Home Appliances: Fridge, washing machine, television set and other home appliances that you buy depreciate in value. Imagine that you bought a fridge for ₹10,000. After one week, you want to sell it for some reason. You cannot sell it above 10,000 or even for the same 10,000. You can sell it only below 10,000, because these appliances depreciate—decrease in value. That is why taking a loan to buy home appliances is bad debt and must be avoided.

People time and again ask what the harm is in going for 0 percent EMI to buy an appliance, as there is no interest outflow. 0 percent EMI is the driving force behind many of the purchase decisions nowadays. 0 percent EMI makes people buy things they cannot afford. Soon, it becomes a habit to buy in 0 percent EMI and people end up paying multiple EMIs, eating up a huge portion of their salaries. But, do you know that the 0 percent EMI was banned by the Reserve Bank of India (RBI) in 2013? In its circular dated September 17, 2013, it stated that the very concept of 0 percent interest is non-existent.

How do these schemes still work then? The interest cost is in some way passed on to customers either in the form of processing fees or in the form of denying offers and discounts. If you pay cash up front, you get a better negotiation power and a better deal.

The main business of banks or any other financial institution is to give loans and earn interest. Interest is their bread and butter. Will they forego their income? They will not. The name of the interest changes, the effect does not.

Mobile Phones: Every day, new models of mobile phones are launched to attract customers. One of the most popular lifestyle-related devices is a mobile phone. People are ready to spend even one lakh rupees to buy a new phone. Many times, they do not have much cash in hand and so take loans. The purchase decision for a mobile phone is often driven by the heart and not by a smart mind. The costliest phone comes with loads and loads of features. Seldom do we use those features. Then, why to spend so much money to buy something that we don't use? Also, these mobile phones depreciate — decrease in value. Taking loans to buy a mobile phone is bad debt and must be avoided.

Cars: Should I not take a loan for a car? YES. You should NOT. Many people think it is absurd because a car loan is one of the popular loans today.

Let us do a simple math. You take a car loan for five lakhs. The average car loan interest rate is 9.25 percent per annum. The maximum number of years in which you can repay is seven years for a car loan. Your monthly EMI, in this case, will be 8108/- and you will end up paying 6.8 lakhs. Here are two things to observe: 1) You end up paying 1.8 lakhs as interest, which is 35 percent of your car value. 2) Friends, your car will not be worth 6.8 lakhs at the end of seven years.

Now, you tell me: Is it wise to take a car loan?

Wondering, how to buy a car without taking a loan?

Here is what my friend Arjun did. Not knowing how to drive a car, he did not want to buy a new car and dent it everywhere. It would be heartbreaking to see dents and scratches on your new car. Isn't it? So, he bought a Maruti 800 second-hand for ₹50,000. After one year, Arjun became well-versed in driving and thought of upgrading his car. He had only 2.5 lakhs in savings, which might not have been enough to buy a new car. He decided to wait for one more year and save more money. He lived with his Maruti 800, and at the end of the second year, he had five lakhs in savings. Then, he started looking for cars within five lakhs. That was when he found out about Hyundai exchange mela, for Ganesh Chaturthi. He took his Maruti 800 and asked for the exchange rate. To his surprise, his car was priced at ₹65,000, including the exchange bonus of ₹40,000 given to him at a table profit of ₹15,000 for buying the car only at ₹50,000. Are you able to follow? He purchased a brand new Grand i10 for ₹5,65,000, with the money he had in hand five lakhs plus the money that he got by exchanging his old Maruti 800, ₹65,000. Isn't that wise? The best part was that Arjun did not need to pay any EMI from the next month. He did not end up taking a bad debt. Even after hearing Arjun's story, you may not be willing to wait. That is primarily because we are in the era of instant gratification. We want instant responses to our Facebook posts, Instagram stories. We do not want to wait because the instant gratification gives you a boost, makes you feel happy.

Please be aware of good debts and bad debts. If you are taking a loan for an investment that will grow in value, then it is a… good debt; go for it. If you are taking a loan for anything that will NOT grow in value, like your car, home appliances, then it is a… bad debt; please do not go for it.

–V–

Debt Trap

Beware of bad debts and do not get into a debt trap.

What is a debt trap?

Do you remember my uncle who kept on using his credit card for shopping and paid only a minimum amount due? Yeah! He ended up paying double the amount of what he spent. That is a typical debt trap. A debt trap is a situation that favors the lender/banker strongly, not you. You end up paying an unreasonable rate of interest, high penalties, late fees, etc.

To give you one more example of a debt trap: my friend Ashish bought a few shares, earning him a little profit by selling them at a higher price. That little success pushed him to do more. Quite natural, isn't it? He continued buying and selling shares, without proper knowledge about the stock market. That was when another friend suggested him to buy more shares of Ashok Leyland, saying that the share price would double up soon. Ashish was tempted. He wanted to buy those company shares, however, did not have enough cash. Then came this dangerous idea of taking a personal loan and investing in the share market. He calculated interest he must pay and projected the profit he is going to get out of the share market. Ashish found that it is a good idea to get a personal loan and invest in the share market, as its more profitable. He took a personal loan for ₹5 lakhs from a bank and bought shares through and through. The monthly EMI was ₹9,100. Unfortunately, the share market crashed. The prices went down. Ashish could not sell the shares for he would end up in loss. He found it difficult to pay the EMI due to an unexpected turn of events. He skipped a few EMIs. The bank charged him penalties, late fee, cheque return charges and what not. After one year, Ashish's stocks that he had bought for ₹5 lakhs went down to ₹70,000. He ended up paying close to ₹7 lakhs to the bank, including the late fee and other charges Ashish situation is a typical debt trap situation where it favored the lender/banker strongly. *If you have an idea of taking a loan and repurposing it into the share market, please drop that idea.* A lot of things in the share market is not in your control. Financial advisors highly recommend having equity exposure, however that must not be out of borrowed money.

Many have the habit of taking a personal loan to meet their expenses because a personal loan is also a popular type of loans like housing loan and car loan. People take it right and left. Want to get married, take a personal loan. Want to go for a foreign vacation, take a personal loan. Want to buy the costliest mobile phone, take a personal loan. Want to help your friends, family and relatives by giving them money, take a personal loan. It is easy to take a personal loan. There are banks in India which disburse the loan amount in less than 48 hours. But, please remember that interest on a personal loan is anywhere from 14 percent onwards.

–VI–

Most Popular Loans

Before learning how to reduce your loans and EMI, let's see what some of the popular loans offered by banks are, its nature, history, drawbacks and much more. This information may supplement your financial decisions.

a) Housing Loans

One of the most popular loans in India is the housing loan. Almost every salaried person has a housing loan and is paying a huge EMI, irrespective of their affordability. There is too much of social pressure to live in an owned house. The parents also want their wards to buy a house, as soon as they get into a job, so that the money is properly invested and not spent unnecessarily.

The fact is that the people who live in a rented house lead a far happier life than those who live in an owned house. Independent of the ownership of the house, happiness is in fact a mental state. Owning a house, no more brings happiness as most of the owned houses are apartments. The floor is not yours; the roof is not yours; the wall is not yours and you get a small share of the land. If it is an individual house, then it is a different story. However, many prefer apartments as they find it difficult to construct their own house, spending huge money and time. We are in a fast food, instant mix era. We need a house that is being built by someone and we just take the possession. However, in the individual house one must spend time making each decision and shape the house like a potter shapes pots out of clay. That requires a lot of patience and time. But the amount of satisfaction that building an individual house gives is irreplaceable. Whether it is an apartment or an individual house, owning one is a status symbol and exactly why people burden themselves with loans and buy a house on their own.

But, do you know how people bought their own houses in India 40 years ago?

Let me brief you about the growth of the home loan sector in India. Housing loans are only four decades old, approximately 40 years. In the 1970s, there was no concept of "housing loan". Then, how did people buy houses before? People's mentality was to save and purchase. They bought houses from their PF savings and retirement benefits that they would get upon leaving the job. On the contrary, now we see people buying a house as soon as they join a job. HDFC was the only organized loan provider at that time. Now, we have plenty of banks offering housing loans.

How did this change in the last 40 years? Why are there so many high-rise apartments, communities?

Let me brief you the four main reasons:

1. **Free Economy aka Globalization:** When globalization came into practice in 1991, banks started entering the home loan market and started giving many offers. ICICI Bank introduced the floating rate concept in 2000, which was a massive hit. Then, State Bank of India came to the market, a little late, but with a differentiator. They introduced the teaser rate – 8 percent interest for the first year, 9 percent for the next two years and market rates for the rest of the term.

2. **SARFAESI Act 2002:** The introduction of Securitization and Reconstruction of Financial Assets and Enforcement of Security Interest (SARFAESI) Act gave banks the authority to deal with defaulters. Until then, the banks did not have a recovery mechanism.

3. **Interest rates:** The rate of interest was so high up to 14 percent. With the free economy, RBI gave banks the freedom to fix their interest rates. It opened interest war with banks and eventually the interest rates came down.

4. **Government of India** played their part in the growth of the "home loan" sector by giving income tax exemptions for a housing loan. Today, these concessions are one of the main reasons why people go for housing loans.

Due to these four reasons, the home loan sector grew multifold in India in the last 40 years.

b) Credit Card

Another popular and attachable type of loan is a credit card. You may wonder if a credit card is really a loan? You are billed for your purchases, or usage, and are obligated to pay on the due date. Where is the loan part here? The loans on a credit card are revolving credits. You are offered a credit limit that allows you to use money when needed. Banks provision the money up to the extent of your credit limit for you to use. Though you may not be using the entire money in your credit card in a single transaction, the banks ensure that the money is available there for you to use.

Many people have more than one credit card nowadays. Credit cards have penetrated the market manifold in the past four decades. The credit cards found a permanent place in everyone's wallet. Today, in India there are close to 50 million credit card users as of May 2019.

In 1980, the Central Bank of India launched the first bank credit card in India. In 1981, Andhra Bank launched its credit card.

The term "product" was referred only in the consumer durables sector until the late 1980s. This term was then extended to the services sector also. The services offered by banking institutions are referred to as "products".

A credit card is one of the most profitable products of a bank. This product offers multiple ways to a bank to make money.

1) Fee: Membership fee, over-limit fee, transaction fee, balance transfer fee, late fee are some of the fees being charged by banks. Few banks offer free membership cards, most of them charge an annual membership fee. Some banks charge a membership fee and offer to refund if you spend X amount of money within a certain period. An over-limit fee is charged to the customers who exceed their credit limit. A transaction fee is charged in case of transacting in different currencies. Some banks charge a transaction fee for online utility payments such as electricity bills, train ticket bookings, insurance premiums, etc. When you transfer the outstanding balance from one card to another, the banks charge you a balance transfer fee. We see in detail all about balance transfer in the upcoming chapters. Late fee is charged when you fail to make the full payment on or before the due date.

2) Interest: If you do not pay the entire bill amount within the due date, then the interest is charged to the outstanding amount. A higher interest rate is charged due to the convenience, flexibility, and instant access the credit card offers. On an average, credit card companies charge 36 percent to 48 percent per annum as interest on the amount outstanding. Out of all the loan instruments available in the market, credit cards are the most expensive ones.

Fees and interest are the two major ways by which the banks make money out of credit cards. Credit card is a double-edged sword. If used properly, it would help you to reap benefits such as instant money during emergency times, free credit up to 50 days, reward points, etc. Still, unfortunately people do not know how to manage credit cards and end up paying a huge amount as fee and interest to the banks.

Recently, I conducted a survey with a small sample of 100 people out of my contacts. The answers revealed that more than 65 percent of people use more than one credit card. This behavior is worrisome because a credit card is the most expensive debt. At times, it becomes difficult for people to manage the bills and remember the due dates for each of the credit cards. That leads to missing due dates, paying penalties, interests and falling into a debt trap naturally. What started as a tool for emergency for most of them, later turned out to be a disaster. If you are using more than one credit card, you need to be extra cautious. It is important to alter your behavior toward credit card if you do not want to get into a debt trap later. Here are the five golden rules you must follow if you are using a credit card.

1. **Always pay the dues in full:** A credit card in hand would make you behave differently. It would push you to buy things unaffordable within your monthly income. People go ahead and buy expensive items just because they do not need to pay immediately. Credit card companies generate a bill on a day of the month, a due date to make the payment. Once you receive the bill, you must pay the entire amount due. But, at times you might not have the required money as it exceeds your monthly income. In such cases, people tend to pay the minimum amount due or try to *convert* the purchase into an EMI. Both are dangerous and will hurt you in the long run. Never make part payments or the minimum amount due. Paying the minimum amount due is a "MAD" thing. MAD stands for "Minimum Amount Due". Hence, always pay the entire outstanding amount. Else, the bank would charge you late fees, penalty charges and interest on the outstanding amount. The bank that issues the credit card charges anywhere between 36 to 48 percent interest per annum. It will only lead you into a debt trap.

I suggest you execute a standing instruction with your banker to pay, automatically the credit card bills in full. It would give you several advantages. a) You would always make the full amount due, which will automatically be deducted from your bank account. It means that you ensure enough balance in your bank account, which in turn drives you to spend within your monthly income. b) You do not need to keep remembering the due date as the standing instruction will take care of it. Sometimes, forgetting the due date might lead you to the late payment, attracting some charges and a negative credit score. You can avoid all of these by having a standing instruction in place. c) This would save you from falling into a debt trap for you would always make the payments in full. d) Making payments on time month after month would improve your credit score, thereby helping you to take loans for the items that increase in value (i.e. a good debt).

2. **Keep track of your credit card expenses**: It is important to keep track of all your expenses, especially the credit card expenses. What I learned from my friends, colleagues and relatives is that not many are keeping track of their expenses. They either feel lazy or do not see the necessity to maintain a record of their expenses. *Keeping track of your credit card expenses will help you ensure that you are billed only for your spending.* Also, your expenses record will serve you as a reference point in the future. You will find more about tracking expenses in the upcoming chapters of this book.

3. **Read the monthly statement carefully**: As soon as you receive the credit card statement, please read each row item carefully. If you do not know of your purchase from any specific row item, you can crosscheck with your expense tracker. This exercise helps identify errors in the statement such as you are charged for an amount unspent or some miscellaneous charges. In case of errors, you report it, get it rectified and save a few bucks.

I check my groceries bills even. Whenever I buy groceries, electronics, clothes, and so on I always read/check the bills. I preserve those bills for at least 30 days. One day, while I checked my groceries, I found erroneous billing for three items amounting to ₹460. The next day, I went to the shop and reported this issue.

The shop owner immediately accepted the error and returned the money. At times, a simple habit can save your hard-earned money.

Not to say that every statement or every bill would have some errors. However, in the case of credit cards, you must check your monthly bills as it is the most expensive debt instrument. Any additional charges might cost you heavily. Even though it is the responsibility of the credit card companies to produce accurate bills, it's your duty too to validate the bills for accuracy. Consumer law says, 'Buyers beware.' You must be aware of such situations and protect yourself from such erroneous billing situations. In a nutshell, you must develop the habit of reading your monthly statements to identify errors, if any. *The third golden rule for using a credit card is to read monthly statements with the utmost care.*

4. **Do not ever withdraw cash from your credit card,** because interest will be charged from the very next day. There is no free credit period for cash. When I said this in one of my keynote sessions, surprisingly a few people met me after the speech and told me that they did not know this information. First, if you are using any product like a credit card, mobile phones, and so on, you must know all the features or the terms and conditions of that product. It would enhance your experience. I know some of my friends who have high-end cars, but they do not know all the features of the car. There are few keys and buttons untouched in the car even after many years of purchase. Knowing all the features and their use will give you a good, satisfying experience.

Coming back to credit cards, in case of misinformation regarding this, beware of cash withdrawals from your credit card as it attracts interest from day *one*. The free credit period is available only for purchases made using your credit card in the stores/

shopping outlets. The credit period for those purchases is limited until the due date of the bill. Being unaware of a product you use is not bliss. I know many people who have burned their fingers because either they stay unaware of interest from day *one* or they go ahead with blind courage.

In 2012, My friend Anand was advised by someone to buy a plot, a vacant land on the outskirts. He was told of a good investment and price that would go to sky level, along with the proposed airport a few kilometers away from the land. Anand got tempted. He was looking to buy a plot for some time as both his brothers had already bought their own land. His father kept insisting he also buy a vacant land for his future betterment. He thought of buying that land for a good investment. He was even convinced that its price would go up and made up his mind to buy the plot. He asked for the price and was surprised to know the cost: ₹6 lakhs. His budget was only ₹3 lakhs. The person who showed him the land told that the prices are at a premium as with the airport in the locality the prices would soon go up. He also told Anand about the huge demand for the place and otherwise having someone else ready to buy it. The person insisted Anand arrange for the remaining money and invest it there for assured returns.

Anand became restless. He wanted to buy the land for sure but was short of ₹3 lakhs. He could not take a housing loan with that amount for a vacant land as it is. All he had was a credit card. He did some calculations and projections: the hike in the price of the plot in another one year; payment for the credit card; profit after paying the credit card dues. Everything looked so positive to his eyes.

So, he confidently withdrew cash from his credit card and purchased that plot and felt happy with his decision. But, friends, time proved him wrong. The land price did not go up. The airport never came about. Instead, the credit card dues went up. He ended up paying ₹7 lakhs to the credit card and he disposed of the land in 2015, after three years, for ₹7 lakhs – roughly about 16 percent returns in three years. If he would have bought that land from his savings, then the decision is somewhat okay. But he did a mistake by withdrawing cash from the credit card. What lessons do you and I can learn from Anand's experience? Never withdraw cash from a credit card. It will hurt our wallet. Our hard-earned money evades in the name of interest. The bankers do not ask us to do that. It is we who push ourselves into such a terrible situation and burn our fingers. Please be careful while using credit cards. It is a double-edged sword. Never, ever withdraw cash from your credit card.

5. **Do not take another loan to repay your credit card debt:** Many people, when they cannot pay the credit card dues in full, tend to take a loan from another bank to pay their dues. It is not only with credit card loans, but any loan for that matter. They would have taken the loan anticipating earnings. However, when the due date arrives, at times they are not able to source the money and repay. So, naturally, they would take another loan to repay this loan. It might be to get an easy way out. Still, it needs to be done in the right way.

You would not be closing a loan that way, but transferring your loan and paying interest and charges—a debt trap to find yourself in. You may get temporary relief for sure. Still, the act of taking another loan to repay an existing loan would have a cascading effect on your finances. You will get into a loop, wherein you keep performing the same action and find it difficult to come out of the loop.

Also, I have seen many people do a balance transfer. Balance transfer is quite common with credit cards, especially among those who overspend and find no way to pay the credit card bill. It is nothing but transferring the credit card due amount from one card to another card.

For example: You are using an HSBC credit card and have an outstanding amount of ₹20,000. Assume that you do not have the money to repay. You also have a CITI Bank credit card. Then, you call CITI Bank and place a balance transfer request. Within one or two days CITI Bank will process your request. CITI Bank will pay HSBC and show that amount (₹20,000) as an outstanding amount on your CITI Bank credit card statement. There will be a processing fee, but you can escape from the late fee that would have been charged by HSBC otherwise. CITI Bank will allow you 90 days to repay the dues. You need to pay the entire amount of ₹20,000 on or before 90 days. This is how balance transfers work.

Some do balance transfers every 90 days, back and forth, and later end up paying a processing fee equivalent to the outstanding amount. Balance transfer is not the right choice to make as you would be juggling a lot where anyway you have to pay a fee – only you call it differently.

Taking another loan to repay your credit card debt, may give you some relief from the due dates, late fees, penalties in the short term, however in the long run, it will dent your personal finances in a huge manner. You would end up in a debt trap and that is a difficult position to come out of, at times it gets impossible.

Speaking out of experience, I was a proud owner of multiple credit cards and did a lot of balance transfers as there were huge debts to service. I had no choice at that time. With little income and huge debt, the natural choice is to get into more debt. Little discipline and planning will help you come out of debt and stay away from getting into a new loan to repay an existing loan.

Please follow these five golden rules, if you use one or more credit cards. If you think that you cannot follow any of these rules, then please avoid using credit cards. Trust me, this is the best piece of advice you can ever get.

1. Always *pay* the dues in full
2. Keep track of your credit card expenses
3. Read the monthly statement carefully
4. Do not ever withdraw cash from your credit card
5. Do not take another loan to repay your credit card debt

c) Car Loans

Once, in India, every house had a bicycle. The man at home will clean the bicycle and maintain it well. The maintenance cost is almost zero. The kid at home feels pride in sitting on the small seat exclusively made for him. The woman at home occupy the back seat and the bicycle was a complete transport solution for a family. Then came motorbikes, costlier than bicycles. That is when auto loans came into existence. Later, every house owned a motorbike. In the 1990s globalization came in. That saw a surge in income levels. People earned a lot of money, but only to spend. The products that were perceived as luxury turned out to be a necessity. Car is one such product. Fast forward 2020, almost every house has a car. Many houses do not even have a space to keep cars. Irrespective of that, people went and bought cars. People seldom realize that the actual spending starts only after buying a car. The maintenance expenses are way too high for cars. Fuel, insurance, service charges, repair expenses take a reasonable portion out of your annual income.

Banks are ready to give loans to buy a car. The car loan business in India sees an annual growth of 18-20 percent. A car loan interest rate is between 8.5 percent to 10 percent currently. Interestingly, in a country like India where agriculture gives employment to more than 50 percent of the people, with 17-18 percent GDP contribution, the tractor loan interest rate is anywhere between 11-23 percent. Why are car loans cheaper than tractor loans? It should be the other way round. Isn't it?

There are a lot of emotions and pride attached to a car. The middle-class and the upper-middle-class families in India are attached to these emotions and pride. They are ready to buy a car even if they do not have enough money. The demand for cars is also quite high. That is why bank loans are popular and growing at this pace.

A bicycle, a motorbike or a car seems a lifetime purchase. Once you buy a motorbike, it becomes your identity. I know an uncle driving the same motorbike since my childhood. In 2020 the case is different. My friends change the car every five years. Every year, new models of cars are being introduced, almost by every car company. The speed at which the world revolves and products are being introduced pushes consumers to upgrade their cars. This means one person takes a car loan more than once in their life. This is not a healthy sign.

d) Personal Loans

Personal loans are not secured loans, like home loans or car loans. They are unsecured loans. You do not need to give any collateral security to get a personal loan. The banks do not have any asset-backed security to recover loans in case of non-repayment. They can only proceed with legal actions. Due to this nature, banks charge a higher rate of interest for personal loans. The average interest rate for a personal loan is above 14 percent. In western countries, credit score plays a role in determining interest rates for a personal loan. Higher the credit score, lower the interest rate. In the eyes of a lender, a high credit score means less risk. In India, banks use credit scores only as eligibility criteria. It does not influence interest rates. Alternatively, an Indian borrower can compare interest rates from various banks to find out the cheapest one.

People take personal loans to meet their needs unmet otherwise. Personal loans are taken for marriage expenses, emergency needs, exotic holidays, medical expenses, repaying another loan and maternity expenses.

Banks easily make available and quickly process personal loans. Because of this, a personal loan is a popular choice among people when they need money. You would have noticed someone issuing pamphlets at the entrance of huge buildings where many people work. You would have also received phone calls from tele-callers asking if you need a personal loan. Personal loans are targeted mainly to salaried employees for a simple reason that the repayment is almost guaranteed. Salaried employees receive their salaries in a bank account. The banks that lend get cheques or standing instructions executed in that bank account via Electronic Clearing System (ECS) to recover the money.

The advantages of personal loans are: 1) They are unsecured. You do not need to provide any collateral security. 2) Personal loan interest rates are cheaper than credit card rates. 3) You can take personal loans for any need whatsoever. You do not need to state the reason to the bank. Whether marriage expenses or some emergency need, even to repay another loan, you can take a personal loan for all such needs. 4) Personal loans are easily and quickly accessible. Banks take less time to disburse money into your account.

There are also disadvantages of personal loans: 1) Personal loan interest rates are higher than that of secured loans. Banks charge a higher rate of interest as these are unsecured loans. The chances of recovering the loan are less, if in case of non-repayment 2) There is no option to alter the tenure as it is always fixed. Credit card loan tenures are flexible, and you can take as long as you need to repay. 3) There is no prepayment option for personal loans. Other types of loans allow prepaying so that interest burden is reduced. However, personal loans do not provide that advantage. 4) Just because it is easily available and being processed quickly, the decision to take a personal loan is also made quickly.

Ideally, though, one must avoid taking personal loans. Being prepared for unprepared situations is the only way to avoid pitfalls like personal loans.

e) Educational Loans

Educational loans became popular with the raise in school fees. Though banks started giving educational loans in 1995, in 2001 banks adopted it fully. A student can apply for an educational loan to pursue an approved course by recognized universities in native countries as well as abroad. With globalization, came a hike in fees and demand for courses at premier institutes and foreign universities.

In India, for loans up to ₹4 lakhs, no security is required. The parents need to provide collateral security for loans beyond

₹4 lakhs. Banks offer a moratorium period (holiday period) for loan repayment. Students need not repay it during the course plus for a period of about a year and half. However, interest will be accrued for the complete duration and students have a choice to pay interest during the moratorium period. Interest rates on educational loans range from 11-13 percent. Educational loans are a revolutionary step toward making unaffordable education affordable.

Earlier, when the parents did not have enough money to enroll their ward for a course, they would do either of these: 1) They would enroll their ward to a different course that they can afford, a complete mismatch for the student's capabilities most of the times. 2) The parents would borrow money from friends, relatives, or pledge gold (if they have any). 3) The parents avail personal loans, which come with a hefty interest rate (14 percent and above).

I advocate a debt-free life. Still, I would highly recommend taking educational loans. The reason is simple: It is a good debt and will help to uplift not only the student, but also the entire family and the generations to come.

There are counter-arguments that the probability of getting a good job is less, and in case you do not get a good job, then the repayment of the loan is going to be harder, like any other loans. I would not agree with this argument, especially when it comes to educational loans. *Where there is a will, there is a way.*

I started my career as a temporary staff in a nationalized bank and was paid ₹100 every day. No paid leaves, no additional benefits. If I showed up at work, I would get paid. That was how it started. I took up the job, rolled up my sleeves, with only one goal in my mind to become a permanent employee at that bank. I always showed up as the first person in the morning, even before the bank opened and was always the last person to leave for home in the evening. I did not shy away from any small task thrown at me. Looking at my determination to get on permanent payrolls, one of the officers in the bank recommended me for an opening at Standard Chartered Bank. I appeared for the interview and by god's grace I cleared it too. I could not have words to express how I felt. It was a game-changer in my life, which became possible just because I did not wait for a perfect job. I took up the job readily available though it paid me less. The elevation happened organically. Zig Ziglar says, 'You don't need to be great to start, but you need to start to be great.' If you do not get the job you like the most, do not waste time. Grab a job available, get started and pursue your dream job. If a student does that, there is no question of not getting a job. The student will be an employee or an entrepreneur in no time, encouraging them to start the education loan repayment.

–VII–

How to Reduce Loans?

Now, you have got to know why debts are dangerous – what is good debt, what is bad debt and what a debt trap is. Here comes two important questions, the core points in this book. These two questions would naturally ring in one's mind striving hard to come out of debts. In economics, there are two concepts: "willingness" and "ability". Willingness without ability is of no use. Similarly, ability without willingness does not suffice. One may have a willingness to come out of debt but may not know the ways to achieve it. That is why they fall into a debt trap and at times take extreme steps due to their inability to repay debts. There is another category of people who have the ability to repay but they do not want to. They would cheat banks and lenders. This book is not for them.

The focus is on people who are willing to repay but do not have the ability. They will always have these two important questions in their mind.

1. How to reduce my loans and have Zero EMI?

2. How to avoid taking loans for my urgent big expenses, so that I continue to have Zero EMI?

The whole idea of writing this book is to address these two questions. I wanted to share what I had learned not only from my experience, but also from the experience of people I knew. I am completely aware of the practical difficulties of getting rid of the debts. I started my career with a bag full of debts too heavy for me at that age. That was not my choice, though. What I got was a huge responsibility and a burden at the same time. All the responsible family people take loans in order to run their families, not for their self-pleasure. There will always be family welfare behind it.

I have already walked the path full of debts. Believe me, it is not only hard but also tiring. I strongly believe that my experience and learnings can help fellow human beings come out of the debt trap. Each one can start leading a debt-free life and attain financial freedom like me.

In order to achieve financial freedom, the debt-free way, you need to know the answer to two important questions. Let us see one by one.

First, how do you **reduce your loans and have Zero EMI**? You can do it in three ways.

1) **Repay** – The most simple and straightforward method to reduce loans is to repay your loans regularly in an organic way. If you keep paying your EMIs, your loan will get reduced automatically. This is no rocket science.

The banker will give an amortization schedule when a loan is disbursed. The schedule will show the EMI amount, rate of interest, number of months (tenure) and the last EMI month/year. This gives you a complete picture of your loan account. Nowadays an ECS approval is obtained from the borrower to recollect the monthly installments. In simple words, cheques are replaced with ECS when it comes to EMIs. Every month the bank will present the ECS to your bank for collection. You ensure to have enough balance to honor the ECS request so that your EMI is paid duly. When you do this month after month, your outstanding number of EMIs gets reduced, and over a period, you would have repaid all the EMIs and closed the loan.

It may sound like teaching alphabets to a higher secondary student. However, there are times when people struggle to repay EMIs on time. Why is it so? Because of a lack of planning. At times, we encounter an unexpected expense for which we are unprepared. Immediately we think about taking a loan to meet up expenses because it may be something you cannot postpone and needs attention immediately. We would make some calculations in our minds for the repayment. Then, we will go ahead and apply for a loan.

When someone applies for a loan, they would have certain plans in mind to repay the loan. The bank, after receiving the loan application form, would check the income of the applicant to ensure if the person can repay the loan or not. That is why the banks ask for the payslip of the last three months. Also, the bank checks for existing EMIs/loans running by looking at the bank statements. While collecting the application form, that is why the banks insist on three or six months' statements. So, the banks take all precautionary steps to verify the eligibility of the applicant to get an assurance that the borrower will repay the money.

When it comes to the borrower—that is you and me—we pay EMIs regularly and close the loan promptly most of the time. There are also times, we struggle to pay our EMI. There may be various reasons. You would have encountered another unexpected expense during the same tenure. It may be a sudden medical expense you cannot postpone. The annual school fee is another huge, bulk payment that needs to be made. When you do not have money, automatically you go and apply for another loan. That is how people slowly get into a debt trap. Taking up additional loans puts a lot of pressure on you when it comes to repayment. Though paying EMIs and reducing loans is not open-heart surgery, many people struggle to do that simple act because many things can happen in the tenure of one year or two to five years, you end up defaulting EMIs, attracting penalties and landing in a messy situation. How one can avoid defaulting and perform the simple act of paying regular EMIs successfully? It needs some discipline. Financial discipline is an act of taking control of your spending and saving for the plans or goals you have set for yourself. The plans and goals change as the priorities and situations change. Nevertheless, controlled spending and mandatory savings would help one to implement their plans successfully, which again is quite simple. The key is that you must follow it. Write down your monthly income, which is fixed most of the time for the salaried people. So, the advantage is that it is easy to do the math. Below that, write down your monthly mandatory payments. For example: The rent, housing EMI, maid's salary, electricity bill, etc. On deducting the mandatory payments from the income. You will get a certain number. From that amount, allocate a certain percentage for savings even before spending or making plans for expenditure. Now, the remaining amount is available for you to spend for that month. You must control your expenditure during that amount strictly.

At times, the money may not be enough to meet all the expenses for the month. You need to be a little creative by either increasing your income or reducing your expenses. Check for even the smallest way to get an additional inflow of money.

Let me tell you one tiny thing I did during the crisis I faced to get some additional money. You would get an idea of what I am talking about. Whenever I pay at the grocery shop or vegetable shop, there is some balance money that they will return. It may be currency notes or coins. I do not like to keep coins in my wallet, so I collect them in a small box as soon as I reach home. Over a period, the box fills up. I use it when I need money badly and do not have the luxury of leaving those coins in the box forever. Having noticed a regular grocery store manager telling one of his customers that he does not have any coins and getting change is a big challenge, I approach the store person. I tell him that I have some coins and can give him in exchange for currency notes if he needs it. To my surprise, he offers to pay me ₹10 for every ₹100 worth of coins. I immediately rush to my house to check how many coins I have. I find coins worth of ₹3000. With no further delay, I go to the store, give him the coins, and collect ₹300 as a reward. This may be a small amount, but definitely bigger than zero and helped me manage one month's milk expenses at that time. *Do you get what I'm saying? It is an example of an additional inflow of money.* You can think of your own creative ways to bring the extra cash home.

There are plenty of opportunities hidden. We need to discover them. In the book *Ikigai*, which speaks about longevity among people who live in Japan, recommends people to have multiple sources of income. If you are too dependent on a single source of income, then you are fragile, and chances of breaking are high when that source of income stops. If you have multiple sources of income, you would not be stressed even if one of the income sources stops delivering. Find out your passion and explore how you can make money out of it. Create a secondary source of income.

If you are a salaried person, put your 100 percent of effort into your work, especially at times of crisis. It may be difficult because you are already under huge stress and your mind has thoughts around repaying loans. You can consider upgrading your skills so that you get a competitive edge at your workplace. When you put your 100 percent efforts at work and at the same time upgrade, chances of growing up and getting promoted are high. And, you go home with a pay hike. The increased salary helps you save more and be a little lenient on spending.

You can think about your own ways of increasing your income and reducing expenses that will help you to lead a financially disciplined life. If you achieve that, then the simple act of repaying EMIs regularly and reducing the loans is no more a rocket science, no more an open-heart surgery. It is a simple and straightforward way to reduce your burden.

2) **Prepay** – Many banks or lenders allow you to prepay your loans, meaning you can make part payments in addition to your EMIs. Those part payments are adjusted toward your principal outstanding amount. You have a choice to either reduce the loan term to end up paying the loan faster and get away from it. *You may think, 'I don't have anything left out after paying my EMIs. Where would I go for money to prepay?'* You need to remind yourself that when there is a will, there is a way. It may sound philosophical, but

it is a fact. Most of the companies pay an annual bonus, a lump sum amount every year. What do you do with that money? You can use that money to prepay your loans. Once you do not have any loan to pay for, the annual bonus is all yours to spend.

All you must do is keep track of what is coming and what is going. Only then, you will know what is left. Here comes an important question: Do you track your expenses? One important powerful habit I have learned from my father during my early 20s is to write down the expenses incurred. Every day before he goes to bed, he would sit and write down that day's expenses in a notebook. I have imbibed this habit somehow and follow it till now. This helps me to track my expenses and understand "where my money is going". Habits are powerful. A single habit helps me to know how much would be left at the end of every month, every year. It helps me to plan for my housing loan prepayment.

As a housing loan takes almost 60 percent to 70 percent of the monthly income in most cases, let us see how to reduce housing loans. For example: I took a housing loan of ₹45 lakhs for 20 years. The EMI was ₹43,340. I started saving money wherever possible. I used my savings to prepay the housing loan. With such measures, I closed the housing loan in 10 years. I saved 10 years or 120 months of EMI worth ₹52 lakhs (120 x 43,340). *Isn't it huge?* Before I tell you how I did that, let us see how you can prepay your housing loan and come out of it faster.

Let us take another example. Shilpa took a housing loan of ₹30 lakhs to buy a small apartment in her neighborhood. She went for a 20-year loan period. The bank charged her 10 percent interest rate. The EMI was fixed at ₹28,951.

Loan Amount	30 Lakhs
Tenure	20 Years
Interest	10 Percent
EMI	28,951

Shilpa paid 69.50 lakhs at the end of 20 years. 39.50 lakhs more than what she had borrowed. As you all know, it is the interest component.

Principal	₹30,00,000	Start Date	2019 June
Interest	₹39,48,156	End Date	2039 May
Total	**₹69,48,156**	Total Tenure	20 Years

We all know it is impractical or highly impossible for someone to pay lakhs of rupees from their savings to buy a house. Naturally, we would get into a housing loan. But housing loans also come with a lot of pitfalls. It locks us or makes us committed for a certain amount every month, which we have not earned yet. For the rest of the loan period, the borrower ensures a steady monthly income to repay the loan. This brings up a lot of pressure and in turn will stress the person. The stress will have a ripple effect on the entire family. There is no choice as it is not possible to save money and then buy a house. Also, there is a pressure from the society or peers due to which people buy a house. In the olden days, people would buy the house only after retirement. Today the scenario is different. The house was bought, within the very first year of employment. People buy a house or property to save tax, for which they get tax exemption from paying the principal and interest amount every year. There is another aspect when it comes to buying a house. People think that instead of paying the monthly rent, they can pay EMI to have the house become theirs over a period. The truth is that the EMI amount is never equal to the rent one would pay for a house. It is always higher than the rent amount. Still, people stretch their expenses to buy their own house.

Whatever may be the reason for buying a house, people are buying their own houses. As we saw in Shilpa's example, the interest amount is more than the principal amount. It is really a worrying concern. The good news is that there are techniques to repay loans faster and reduce the burden of interest to a great extent. if you follow some techniques, you can repay your housing loan faster and save a lot of your hard-earned money. Let us see some of the techniques one by one.

Technique 1

Shilpa got a salary rise and she was so happy. She told her family members, and everyone wanted to celebrate with her. The ideas started pouring. Her husband wanted to go for a family vacation. Her kids wanted to buy a gaming console, but Shilpa had other plans. She said to her husband and her kids that she was going to use the extra money to increase the housing loan EMI. Obviously, the family was upset because there was no joy or pleasure in paying an extra amount to the bank. No instant gratification. Shilpa made them understand that they can go for a vacation and buy a gaming console once their loans are finished. She immediately wrote to her banker to increase the housing loan EMI. She started paying an additional amount of just ₹3000 every month. That small additional amount every month helped Shilpa finish her loan in 15.3 years instead of 20 years. Instead of ₹28,951, she paid ₹31,951, which **reduced 4.5 years of the loan tenure and saved close to ₹11 lakhs.**

Technique 1 (3000 extra every month)			
Principal	₹24,51,000	Start Date	2019 June
Prepayments	₹5,49,000	End Date	2034 Oct
Interest	₹28,83,455	Total Tenure	15.3 Years
Total	₹58,83,455		

Technique 2

Shilpa was excited to know about her savings by just paying ₹3000 extra every month. She wanted to repay more and see how much more she could save. Instead of paying ₹ 3000 every month, she decided to save money and pay ₹15,000 once in three months. She can also pay ₹5000 every month, however her monthly expenses were slightly fluctuating. So, she made a point to save money every month, and at the end of three months she started paying ₹15,000 to her banker. Shilpa, by using this technique, finished her loan in 13.5 years instead of 20 years. She saved 6.5 years and ₹14.5 lakhs just by paying 15,000 extra once in every three months. When compared to the first technique, it amounts to two years and ₹3.5 lakhs more in savings. All that Shilpa did was: instead of paying ₹3000 every month she started paying ₹15,000 once in three months. There is a popular saying: 'Necessity is the mother of invention.' So, when a person has a necessity and an objective to reduce loans faster, then he or she becomes creative at finding solutions.

Technique 2 (15,000 extra once in 3 months)			
Principal	₹22,05,000	Start Date	2019 June
Prepayments	₹7,95,000	End Date	2032 Dec
Interest	₹24,95,739	Total Tenure	13.5 Years
Total	₹54,95,739		

You would be excited if I say that you can save much more money than this and prepay it faster. Shilpa also got excited when she uncovered the third technique.

Technique 3

When the student is ready the teacher appears. Shilpa was always looking for ways to find an extra amount that she could use to prepay her loan. ₹15,000 once in every three months came to ₹60,000 every year. Shilpa decided to go beyond that. She thought deeply and made use of the annual bonus to repay the housing loan. The annual bonus, otherwise, was meant to meet some of the ad-hoc, unplanned expenses. So, she decided to make a proper plan to use the annual bonus in a meaningful way. Settled on paying an additional amount of ₹1 lakh every year with the help of the annual bonus, she was able to finish her loan in less than 11.5 years instead of 20 years. It saved her 8.5 years and 18 lakhs just by paying one lakh extra every year.

Technique 3 (₹1 lakh extra every year)			
Principal	₹19,00,000	Start Date	2019 June
Prepayments	₹11,00,000	End Date	2030 Dec
Interest	₹21,14,240	Total Tenure	11.5 Years
Total	₹51,14,240		

By moving from **technique 2** to **technique 3**, Shilpa was able to save two years of EMI and close to ₹4 lakhs more.

Isn't it awesome? You save lakhs of rupees just by proper planning and securing some funds. Shilpa saved money, prepaid her loan, and finished repayment faster.

There is another way to finish loan payments quickly. You can take it as a bonus.

The bank offers two types of interest: Fixed and floating. You would have chosen it while signing up for the loan. If your loan is under a floating rate of interest, then you must periodically check with your banker/lender about the current interest rate. If the current rate is lower than the interest rate you pay, then ask your banker to rewrite your loan to a newer rate of interest.

The bank interest rates came down recently, especially during the Covid-19 period. Though banks would say it is a floating rate of interest, they seldom reduce the rates on their own. It needs a request from the borrower to reduce interest. Most of the banks/lenders would reduce interest rates if requested. By doing so, your EMI amount would come down or the number of EMIs (loan tenure) are reduced. I did this regularly with LIC Housing Finance Limited (LICHFL). They always obliged to reduce the interest rate. It helped me finish my housing loan faster.

3) Restructure – Now, the third important and crucial way to reduce your loans. The two ways that we know: Repay and prepay. However, there is also another way of which many are unaware. This method comes in handy when there is an absolute cash crunch with multiple debts and the person is deeply caught in the debt trap. Restructuring debts would give some relief and breathing time to recover from them. Let us see how Gautam did it.

Gautam is my neighborhood friend, and I know him since our childhood. After shifting my house, we could not meet often. The last time I met him during his marriage, a year ago. I accidentally saw Gautam at a supermarket. He looked so worried. The happiness or glow of a newly married guy was missing. My mind started thinking of the reasons for his worry. Was it his marriage life? Was it some job-related issues? Was he unwell? I could not resist asking him: 'Why are you looking so dull, Gautam?'

Hesitating a lot, he opened his Pandora's box of debt. I was shocked to listen to his story. Gautam was in a debt trap. He had 12 lakhs of loans without any asset to back it up. All of them are unsecured, bad debts. He had a deficit/shortage of ₹20,000 every month. He was managing the deficit somehow by rotating money here and there. He could pay a few EMIs and was unable to pay the remaining. So, the non-payment of EMIs attracted late fees, penalties, and the debt began to pile up.

Friends, what will you do in such a situation? What solution or suggestion could you give to Gautam?

I suggested him to restructure his entire debt into manageable chunks. Debt restructuring is quite common for companies. Restructuring involves altering the entire loan schedule in a way that the individual can afford to pay. This will help the individual to get a discount on interest or at times a waiver. The tenure of the loan can be altered by reducing the EMI so that the burden comes down. It is a win-win situation for both the banks/lenders and individual borrowers. Individuals get some relief and help to come out of the debt trap. Banks also get benefited as they are able to collect some money against no money, otherwise it would have been defaulted by the borrowers. Once the loan is restructured, the bank will issue a new loan schedule.

So, the next obvious question you might have would be: How did we restructure Gautam's loan?

I visited his house on a pleasant Sunday morning. After chatting for a while with his family, we went inside a room with a notebook and a pen. Firstly, we sat down and took a stock of his entire debt. We listed all the related details: The bank name and the nature of the loan—whether it was a personal loan or a credit card outstanding or something else. We also collected details about the interest rate, the principal amount paid, the outstanding principal and the number of months left. Gautam never had such a list. All he did was simply repay some and default some. He did not have a holistic view of his debt as he lost track due to multiple debts. Once he got to see the holistic picture, his face showed some signs of clarity and relief. He never attempted or thought of listing down all his debts. So far, he was shooting in the dark. Having the complete details, he got a lot of clarity about the problem he was fighting to overcome.

In the notebook we were listing the details, I asked him to jot down the income he had. He wrote down his monthly salary. I asked if he had another income, however small it may be. It could be either a rental income, or interests from banks, dividends from shares, or any other regular incomes. Most of the times, people think that the salary is their only income and forget to consider other sources. It does not matter however small it is. Any small amount can contribute to overcoming the mountain of debt. Gautam did not have many additional sources of income, and so we came to an end of the exercise that we were doing. We then got a complete picture of his debts and income. Gautam had three personal loan EMIs running and had credit card dues to five banks plus an overdraft from his savings bank account—overall nine EMIs.

I, then, asked him to list his monthly expenses, to be met, whether he had money or not. For example, house rent, petrol for the two-wheeler, groceries, maid salary, etc. After quickly listing down such unavoidable, mandatory, and recurring expenses, I asked him to provision some money toward "miscellaneous expenses". Gautam wondered and asked me why. I explained to him that he needs to allocate some money to meet emergency expenses that cannot be postponed, like doctor fees, home appliances and two-wheeler repair charges, marriage gifts, etc. He realized the importance of such needs and allocated ₹2000 every month toward miscellaneous expenses. I told him not to repurpose that amount in case he did not have any such expenses during a month. He must allow that amount to accrue to build the ability to meet expenses above ₹2000 in the forthcoming months.

So, the list was ready. It gave a picture of his debts, income, and monthly expenses clearly. Then, income minus monthly expenses were what Gautam had in his hands to repay his debt. *Right?* He needs to manage his debt repayments within that limit. Still, he was with a deficit of ₹20,000 and that was where the whole problem was.

The thumb rule in debt management is: If you have multiple loans, you must knock off the most expensive debt first. Credit card loans are the most expensive of the lot. We approached banks one by one, explaining the adverse financial situation of Gautam, brought to their notice how much Gautam had already paid despite his situation, told them Gautam was still willing to repay, however his ability to do so was weak. The proposal that we made to the banks was: Freeze the principal outstanding amount and do not charge interest anymore. For example, there was a personal loan of ₹2 lakhs for five years, at an EMI of ₹4,811. Gautam, by then, had paid 12 EMIs already. So, the remaining amount outstanding was ₹2.31 lakhs—₹1.71 lakhs of principal outstanding and ₹60,000 of interest outstanding. We requested the bank to freeze the principal outstanding amount of ₹1.71 lakhs and allow Gautam to pay in five years' term—that is in 60 equal installments. It would work out to ₹2,850 when compared to ₹4,811, the earlier amount. 40 percent less straightaway from one loan.

We worked on each loan with each bank to restructure loans into manageable bits. It was not easy to convince the banks as they have no obligation to restructure your loans. They refused, rejected, and resisted Gautam's restructure proposal. We did not give up but went to the bank's main branch in the city and gave our proposal. We sent registered posts to their regional offices, head offices and to the RBI. We kept trying. I asked Gautam to send the same proposal to the Banking Ombudsman in a registered post. Banking Ombudsman is a senior official appointed by the RBI to address customer grievances related to banking services. There are only a handful of Banking Ombudsmans in India. I think there are 20 Banking Ombudsman appointed by the RBI as of 2017. As the number of Ombudsmans is limited, the number of complaints they can handle is also limited. Hence, the RBI established a cadence to lodge a complaint with Banking Ombudsman. One can file a complaint with the Banking Ombudsman if the reply is not received from the concerned bank within a period of one month from the date of complaint. There may be cases wherein the concerned bank would have replied, however the reply was unsatisfactory to the customer. In such cases also the customer can reach the Banking Ombudsman.

We also waited for one month to get a reply from the banks. Then only we reached the Banking Ombudsman.

Surprisingly, many banks called within a few days of sending the restructuring proposal. We got varied responses. Some banks refused the proposal. Some asked for a little time to get back to us. Some did not send any response. In the meantime, Gautam stopped paying all the EMIs. He indicated in his letter to the banks that he would start repaying after his loans are restructured and requested to give him a holiday period for the repayment until the loans are restructured. However, he received phone calls from collection agents asking him to pay the EMI dishonored. Gautam told all of them that he had approached their banks to restructure his loans and he is willing to share a copy of the letter with them, if required. These are some of the practical difficulties during the process of restructuring loans.

After six long months of tireless efforts, we were able to restructure all the loans successfully.

Gautam got a huge relief from his monthly over-commitment. He ended up having ₹6000 in surplus every month against a shortage of ₹20,000 before they were restructured.

There are flip sides to this as well. One is the collection agent's follow-ups, as mentioned earlier. Another is that it will take a toll on your Credit Information Bureau (India) Limited (CIBIL) report, as the banks treated loans as either "settled" or "restructured". However, consistent on-time repayments and good credit habits helped Gautam build a positive CIBIL report. The entire story of meeting Gautam and loan restructuring efforts happened in 2009. Five years later, in 2014, Gautam went on to buy a new house by getting a housing loan from LIC Housing Finance because of the relief from his debts restructured.

Friends, many do not know that something like restructuring can be done and we can go and negotiate with banks. Yes, you can negotiate with banks if you are truly struggling to repay your debts.

Before moving on to the next chapter, let me recap the three ways to reduce your loans and have Zero EMI.

1. **Repay**
2. **Prepay and**
3. **Restructure**

–VIII–

How to Avoid Loans?

It is also important to know how to avoid loans, stay at Zero EMI and be preventive. Prevention is better than cure. There are two categories of people: 1) People who had Zero EMI to pay; 2) People who had EMIs but reduced them to Zero EMI by following the techniques stated in the chapter above. Whichever category you may fall in, this chapter will help you continue to stay at Zero EMI.

Recently, I rolled out a questionnaire asking people questions around debt. The survey was taken by more than 100 people. IT professionals, students, professors, and entrepreneurs took this survey.

Many people agreed that salary increments are not helping them stay away from debt. Most of them vouched for proper savings, reducing expenses, and leading a frugal life to avoid loans.

I was so happy that people are wise and aware of the debt trap. Still, they end up falling into it. They end up taking many loans. *Why is it so?* People take loans for emergency needs like medical expenses, unforeseen situations like job loss, to meet up huge expenses like marriage, etc.

I was thinking aloud. What can one do to handle such situations? How can they mobilize funds to meet huge expenses and handle tough situations?

You can face such emergency situations with ease if you are prepared beforehand. Preparation is the key.

But, when should we start preparing? The time to get prepared is NOW. You need to be prepared when you are absolutely in a normal situation, as well as when you are getting your regular monthly income.

There are five *tips* I can share with you in this book in order to get prepared and sail through unforeseen situations.

1. Create a Budget

Do you have a monthly or a yearly budget? It is an old school technique that gives a view of how much money is coming and what is going out. In other words, you take stock of your income and expenses.

When you are taking stock of your income, do not consider your pay cheque as an income. Think about what other sources of income are there apart from your pay cheque. It may be the interest from your deposits, rent for the house you have let out, etc. Many times, people consider *only* their pay cheque as an income. You may be receiving money from other sources as well. What about your annual bonus? Divide it by 12 and add it to your monthly income. Factor all of them and arrive at your total income.

Next is the expense you make. Budgeting will help you lay out all your expenses and figure out how much you need to feed your family for a month, for three months, for six months, etc. To create a budget, you must know what is coming and what is going. Do you track your expenses? Do you know how much you spend every month; how much you pay toward your bills every month; how much you pay toward your loans every month? All of these put together is your total monthly expense.

As stated earlier, one important powerful habit I have imbibed from my father, during my early 20s, is to write down all expenses. When you write down your expenses, you create data points for yourself. This data comes handy to forecast your future expenses and be prepared for any uncertainty. You know how much you need every month. You do not need to panic, because you have the real data. For this, you need to know how much you spend month after month. Start writing down your expenses every day if you are not doing it already. Nowadays, you do not even need to write down expenses like in the olden days. You have apps. I am not talking about automatic apps that need zero touches. Those automatic apps read the messages from your bank to help you track your expenses. No, I would not talk about those apps as they may hurt your privacy. So, I suggest not to use them. You can browse the app stores to select an app that suits you the most. You can use some simple apps wherein you manually enter your expenses every day.

In a nutshell, create a budget. Take stock of your income and expenses. It will help you to find out how much you need to run your family.

2. Cut Down Your Expenses

Now, you know your expenses because either you are already tracking, or you are going to start tracking. At the end of the month, see what expenses you can get rid of. All impulsive, unessential spending goes out of the door. Be frugal. Spend less wherever possible. I am not saying you be stringent. Do not get that wrong.

When I started my career, I was already soaked in loans. I had multiple bills to pay. The loans not only occupied my wallet but also my mind.

When it came to reducing expenses, I personally took every possible step to reduce my expenses.

My office was nine kilometers away from my house at that time. I was going to the office in a two-wheeler. I stopped taking my two-wheeler and started using public transport, because it was cheaper than a two-wheeler. While taking public transport, I realized that there are different fares for different types of buses. There were ordinary buses with ordinary fare and deluxe buses with deluxe fares. I stopped using deluxe buses as they cost more and waited for ordinary buses to travel. This helped me keep my expenses at bay. I did not buy new clothes for almost three straight years. I managed with what I already had. Going to the theater to watch movies was a big NO at that time. I skipped attending marriage functions that demanded overnight travels to save travel expenses. I never went to restaurants to eat. It also helped save a lot of money. Avoiding all the inessential spending—such as clothing, movies, travel—reduced my expenses. I was left with more money that would have been otherwise spent on inessentials. I used that money to repay my loans fast.

The reason I tell you this story is that "reducing expenses" is the *right thing to do during hardships.*

Similarly, you must look at your expenses and see items *you* can reduce. During the 2020 lockdown, we learned to live with only essential things. Some families lived only with large milk cans from other parts of the world because that was what they got. In Chennai, in my street, we did not see anyone selling vegetables for days together. This period can be used to practice frugal, minimalistic living. By cutting down unnecessary, luxury spending, you end up saving a lot of money. You will be left with more cash in hand, which will in turn help you face tough times comfortably.

So, act *now.* Take stock of unnecessary spending and chop them. Do not show them mercy. But, show them the door.

3. Get Organized

National Association of Professional Organizers (NAPO) statistics states that 15 to 20 percent of the average household budget is spent on buying duplicate items misplaced or lost because of disorganization.

Let me share with you an excellent example that Mahatriaa, a spiritual leader narrated in one of his videos.

Raju was busy getting ready for office, the kids were also getting ready for school. The entire house was like a war zone in the morning. Getting the kids inside the bathroom, dressing them up, making them eat their breakfast, packing their bags, packing his office bags – everything happened within a timeframe of 40 to 60 minutes. Raju and his kids got all set to step out of the house. His hands went to pick the car key and (oops) it was not in its place. The entire family—Raju, his wife, poor kids—started searching for the key in the entire house. They all got tensed and started the blame game. Raju said, 'I gave it to you.' His wife replied, 'You only kept it somewhere.' Raju was unhappy. He said, 'You are always irresponsible.' His wife got upset and told, 'Oh god! You cannot even keep a car key safe; who gave you a job.' Finally, after high, intense drama, Raj found the key and rushed out of the door.

Remember! If your car key is not kept in its place but kept anywhere in the house, as you wish, then it will only add to the chaos. Keeping the key at its place takes a second. If it is done so, then the retrieval of the key also takes a second. 'When you know where your things are, then the retrieval takes just a second.'

Similarly, if you are not well-organized with your financial records, then it will only add to the chaos. It is time to get organized. Collect your documents and put them in one place. Your life insurance policies, health insurance cards, provident fund passbooks, housing loan repayment schedules, housing-tax-related documents, income-tax-related documents, bank account(s) details, statements; all the financial documents that you may have, put them all in order. You can create a space in your cupboard or your table drawer to store these important documents. I know some of my friends use digital lockers to store these documents. I do not use it and so am unable to recommend it. You can analyze the pros and cons of digitally saving your financial documents, especially the security aspects of it, and decide.

Are you well-organized in terms of your financial documents? If not, start being so, because getting organized can help you manifold.

Having everything in one place gives you quick access. It gives you an idea of the financial assistance you can get to manage tough times. In India, you can take loans against your provident fund deposits. Find out your eligibility. Also, you can take loans against your insurance policies. Talk to your insurance agent or the insurance company to find out how much you can avail. The loans against provident fund and insurance may be cheaper than the other loan instruments like credit cards, for which you need to organize your financial documents.

Being organized you know where your keys are and your documents too. Being organized will help you gain a sense of control, reduce your stress, and gain clarity.

4. Build an Emergency Fund

All of us know that we need to build an emergency fund to avoid suffering tough times like recession. Seldom we create such funds. I found from my webinars and speaking events that 90 percent of the participants do not have an emergency fund. Robin Sharma, in his book *The 5 AM Club*, says, 'No idea works until you do the work.' Wishing to have an emergency fund and not acting upon, or not taking steps toward building it will not yield the desired results. A wish will remain a wish, without action.

There are many reasons why people do not build emergency funds. Young people always think that an emergency fund is not required and is meant only for old people. Salaried people wait to get a hike and then start building the emergency fund. When the salary is not enough, they think of other priorities, the need to pay loans, bills, etc. Some people are with the mindset that for emergencies, they would use their credit card. They do not know that using a credit card for emergencies is like getting a free ticket into the lion's mouth. Some are little confident in managing it somehow during an emergency and no preparation is required.

Friends, such mindsets are completely wrong. There should not be any excuse for building an emergency fund.

As a measure to get ready for a recession, job losses or any other unforeseen situations, start building an emergency fund NOW. Treat this as savings for the future. Many people have a mindset that savings are an expense. No, it is not. Savings is not an expense, but a necessity.

You need to know how much you need during the emergency period. It is easy to calculate your monthly expenses and how much you need every month as you are tracking your expenses. The thumb rule formula is: 'your monthly expenses multiplied six times'. Let us call it an X. There is a reason behind keeping it as six months. In case of a job loss or a break in your regular income due to any unfortunate event, you need at least six months of breathing time to start getting your regular income. So, it is kept as six months.

Keep a deadline to build an emergency fund, by which month you would finish building it. If there is no deadline, we all know what happens. If you keep a deadline, the results will be amazing. Let us call this target month as Y.

Now, you know how much is required for your emergency fund, X, and by when you want to finish building this fund, Y. The next step is to set a monthly target to contribute toward this emergency fund. Allocate a fixed amount, let us call it Z. Allocate Z from your salary, every month toward this emergency fund. How do you find out the Z? It is simple. $Z = X/Y$.

If you put the above in a formula:

Total Monthly Expense x 6 = X

Number of months required to build = Y

Monthly allocation = Z (X/Y)

For example, if you want to build an emergency fund (X), say 6 lacs, equal to your monthly expenses six times. Your ETA to build this fund was 12 months (Y). Now, the amount that you must allocate every month (your Z) is 6 lacs divided by 12, which is 50,000 every month.

Total Monthly Expenses x 6 = 1,00,000 x 6 = 6,00,000 (X)

Number of months required to build = 12 (Y)

Monthly allocation = 6,00,000/12 = 50,000 (Z)

Simple math, isn't it?

Now you know how much fund is required for an emergency period. You know the X, Y and Z. The next step is to implement it. Act!

You can park your emergency funds in your savings bank account itself. It will earn a small interest as well. However, the chances of spending that money at the time of need are high. I suggest you open a new bank account for your emergency fund. You can set automatic recurring payment transfers from your salary account to this emergency fund account. In that way, you mandate yourself to build this emergency fund. The chances of you using that amount by mistake is less, as it lies in a different account and maybe in a different bank. The benefits of building an emergency fund are plenty. You feel better as you know that you have an emergency fund to fall back during a crisis. You have a systematic way to build your emergency funds. You will never panic during tough times like job loss, medical emergencies, etc.

5. Stay Away from Loans

You must stay away from loans. That is the way to avoid loans completely. Neglect them. Ditch them. Will Rogers, an American actor turned newspaper columnist quotes: 'Too many people spend money they haven't earned, to buy things they don't want, to impress people they don't like.' He said this almost 100 years ago but holds good even now. Please note that he says that people spend money not yet earned by them. He refers to the loans you take in anticipation that you will earn money in the future and repay. But, your anticipation to earn money in the future may not be met in times of tough situations like a job loss. That is exactly why I ask not to take loans.

Using credit cards is also a type of loan easily available to all of us. Credit cards must be avoided as I told earlier in this book. It is important to alter your behavior toward credit cards because it is the most expensive loan. Staying away from the loans will help you face tough situations comfortably.

Build a new muscle to stay away from loans. Never, ever think of relying on loans for emergency situations. If you do that, then you can avoid taking loans.

Before moving on to the next chapter, let's recap the five tips to avoid loans:

1.   Create a budget.
2.   Cut down unnecessary stuff.
3.   Get organized.
4.   Build an emergency fund.
5.   Stay away from loans.

–IX–

Money Management

Managing money is an art. If you do not manage your money well even after getting into a Zero EMI state, then you will fall back into a debt trap sooner. This chapter is dedicated to understand the advantages of saving money at a much earlier age and know the pitfalls of money mismanagement. It is essential to learn to manage money to stay at Zero EMI.

Sadly, it is not being taught at school. I think it is essential to start teaching about money management to kids, and that is where the solution lies. They grow up without any knowledge or awareness about money. Once they grew up, they straightaway start handling the money they earn, where the mismanagement happens. They learn about money on a trial and error basis and in the due course, they lose their hard-earned money.

The parents will start advising, giving lectures about money once the kids start earning. Just imagine that you started these advises and lectures at a young age itself in the form of education.

What would be the result? The kids will grow as smart kids with complete awareness about money. They will know what to do and what not to do with money. They will turn to be responsible, smart citizens. Such kids will be able to build a stable family life, they will be free out of stress caused due to money issues. Isn't it? If yes, then why don't you start teaching your kids about money?

There is a strong reason why I insist to start teaching about money at a young age. Early education and awareness about money will help the next generation to be well-prepared. They can start saving and investing as soon as they start earning. They must do it with complete awareness and must make well-informed decisions when it comes to investments. Investing at an early age would help reap the benefits of compounding interest. The power of compounding interest is known less. Albert Einstein called compounding interest as "the eighth wonder of the world".

I read an interesting article in Quora by ETMoney, which illustrates the power of compounding interest, beautifully with a coin. Imagine that you are offered one crore rupees in cash or a one-rupee coin that doubles every day for the next 30 days. You are asked to pick any one only. You cannot pick both. Most of us will pick one crore rupees certainly. But you must pick the one-rupee coin that doubles every day for the next 30 days. That one-rupee coin would become 53.5 crores. Please see the table below.

Day	Value of Money
1	1
2	2
3	4
4	8
5	16
6	32

Day	Value of Money
7	64
8	128
9	256
10	512
11	1,024
12	2048
13	4,096
14	8,192
15	16,384
16	32,768
17	65,536
18	1,31,072
19	2,62,144
20	5,24,288
21	10,48,576
22	20,97,152
23	41,94,304
24	83,88,608
25	1,67,77,216
26	3,35,54,432
27	6,71,08,864
28	13,42,17,728
29	26,84,35,456
30	53,68,70,912

This example clearly indicates the power of compounding interest. This one-rupee coin example also teaches the importance of starting to invest early. For example, if you start with the same one-rupee coin from *Day 2*, then it will become only close to 27 crores. 50 percent less of what you would have got if you had started from *Day 1*. Please see the table below.

Day	Value of Money
1	0
2	1
3	2
4	4
5	8
6	16
7	32
8	64
9	128
10	256
11	512
12	1,024
13	2,048
14	4,096
15	8,192
16	16,384
17	32,768
18	65,536
19	1,31,072
20	2,62,144
21	5,24,288
22	10,48,576
23	20,97,152
24	41,94,304
25	83,88,608
26	1,67,77,216
27	3,35,54,432
28	6,71,08,864
29	13,42,17,728
30	26,84,35,456

If you start five days later, then you would have earned only close to 1.7 crores at the end of 30 days. See the table below.

Day	Value of Money
1	0
2	0
3	0
4	0
5	0
6	1
7	2
8	4
9	8
10	16
11	32
12	64
13	128
14	256
15	512
16	1,024
17	2048
18	4,096
19	8,192
20	16,384
21	32,768
22	65,536
23	1,31,072
24	2,62,144
25	5,24,288
26	10,48,576
27	20,97,152
28	41,94,304

Day	Value of Money
29	83,88,608
30	1,67,77,216

This one-rupee coin example clearly indicates the power and value of early investing. Start teaching your kids about the value of saving money early and help them understand the power of compounding interest. If a person invests ₹10000 at the age of 22 and earns a nominal interest rate of 8 percent, he or she would have more than ₹90000 at the age of 50. See the table below.

Age	Beginning of the Year	Interest @ 8%	End of the Year
22	10,000	800	10800
23	10,800	864	11,664
24	11,664	933	12,597
25	12,597	1,008	13,605
26	13,605	1,088	14,693
27	14,693	1,175	15,869
28	15,869	1,269	17,138
29	17,138	1,371	18,509
30	18,509	1,481	19,990
31	19,990	1,599	21,589
32	21,589	1,727	23,316
33	23,316	1,865	25,182
34	25,182	2,015	27,196
35	27,196	2,176	29,372
36	29,372	2,350	31,722
37	31,722	2,538	34,259
38	34,259	2,741	37,000
39	37,000	2,960	39,960
40	39,960	3,197	43,157
41	43,157	3,453	46,610

Age	Beginning of the Year	Interest @ 8%	End of the Year
42	46,610	3,729	50,338
43	50,338	4,027	54,365
44	54,365	4,349	58,715
45	58,715	4,697	63,412
46	63,412	5,073	68,485
47	68,485	5,479	73,964
48	73,964	5,917	79,881
49	79,881	6,390	86,271
50	86,271	6,902	93,173

On the other hand, if you start investing five years later, only from the age of 27, you would have a little over 60000 at the age of 50. That is why it is wiser to start early. See the table below.

Age	Beginning of the Year	Interest @ 8%	End of the Year
22	0	0	0
23	0	0	0
24	0	0	0
25	0	0	0
26	0	0	0
27	10,000	800	10,800
28	10,800	864	11,664
29	11,664	933	12,597
30	12,597	1,008	13,605
31	13,605	1,088	14,693
32	14,693	1,175	15,869
33	15,869	1,269	17,138
34	17,138	1,371	18,509
35	18,509	1,481	19,990
36	19,990	1,599	21,589
37	21,589	1,727	23,316

Age	Beginning of the Year	Interest @ 8%	End of the Year
38	23,316	1,865	25,182
39	25,182	2015	27,196
40	27,196	2,176	29,372
41	29,372	2,350	31,722
42	31,722	2,538	34,259
43	34,259	2,741	37,000
44	37,000	2,960	39,960
45	39,960	3,197	43,157
46	43,157	3,453	46,610
47	46,610	3,729	50,338
48	50,338	4,027	54,365
49	54,365	4,349	58,715
50	58,715	4,697	63,412

As adults, it is our duty to teach kids about the fundamentals of money. I always love the happiness on the kids' faces when I explain the concepts of money and they understand it, during my workshops. They like to learn, but it is us who fail to teach them and have the next generation well-informed.

What will happen if you do not teach your kids about money, its concepts, saving early and the power of compounding interest, etc. They will grow up without any knowledge about money and end up mismanaging it. It may have cascading effects on them and on the people surrounding them. Let me tell you two stories that show the adverse impacts of money mismanagement.

Story #1

Café Coffee Day is a place where I can order coffee and spend loads of time with my friends. I fondly remember those golden times of mine, wherein I had a lot of fun with my friends.

Café Coffee Day is a coffee shop and a chain store. It sells 1.6 billion cups of coffee in six countries. A gentleman named V.G. Siddhartha owns this café chain opened in 1996. The stores offer a quiet place for individuals and groups to sit, relax, talk, and of course have coffee. The experience was completely different. You can take your own time to finish the coffee and leave the place. In a regular hotel, the staff will be behind you asking for new orders or to settle the bill to clear you off quickly and create space for new customers. That is their operating model. Café Coffee Day was a little different. It offered coffee and space. This refreshingly new model, offering coffee in an air-conditioned store with nice ambiance and quiet music became a phenomenal success. Siddhartha went on to open multiple stores in almost all the metros and cosmopolitan cities in India. Later, he expanded outside of India. Also, he successfully integrated forward to become self-sufficient and improve efficiency. They grew their own coffee beans.

The business model of Café Coffee Day was completely new for Indian cities and it became a great success.

Unfortunately, in 2019, V.G. Siddhartha, the founder of Café Coffee Day went missing. Two days later he was found dead in the Netravati river. A letter was found as written by Siddhartha before his death and was published in the media. In that letter, Siddhartha said that he would take responsibility for not creating a successful business model. It was shocking to know that what was perceived as a successful business model from outside was not successful from inside.

This is a story of a successful business that fell into a debt trap and cost a life. In early 2020, Café Coffee Day sold its property for ₹27 billion to repay the debt. This is a true example of money mismanagement and landing into a debt trap, despite a brilliant idea and a successful business model. The money earned must be managed and nurtured to elevate you and the people around you.

Late Mr. Siddhartha has created spaces for others to come, relax and create memories. I felt so bad about him not find a space on this earth longer than his stay. Siddhartha became Gautama Buddha and attained peace and enlightenment. Café Coffee Day founder, Late Mr. Siddhartha chose the other way unfortunately. May he rest in peace.

If you are reading this book, please "reach out" to your friends and family at times of crisis, at times of pressure, at times of deadlock situations; talk to them and vent out.

Similarly, if someone "reaches out" to you to vent out, render your ears and listen to them. Just listen to them, nothing else. Believe me, you are making a difference in their lives.

So, an important responsibility as adults is to teach kids about money. The fundamentals of money—how to earn, manage, save, and grow their money.

Story #2

Vijay Mallya is a businessman with diverse exposure. He was the chairman of United Spirits, the largest alcohol company in India. He is the founder of Kingfisher Airlines. He was the chairman of Bayer, a fertilizer company, for almost 20 years. Vijay Mallya co-founded Force India, a Formula One racing team. He also owned a team in IPL – Royal Challengers, Bangalore. He was even a member of parliament, India.

With such a powerful profile, he was called "the king of good times". He created wealth worth of crores and crores of rupees. But this man was never short of controversies. He led an extravagant, lavish lifestyle. Due to this, he landed in financial troubles. Most of his business ventures went in a loss. On the other hand, he also piled up debts.

Finally, he left India in 2016 and moved to Britain. Approximately 15 banks are trying to collect their dues worth billions of rupees from him. He was filed with many cases including money laundering, cheating, cheque dishonoring and loan default.

Vijay Mallya's story from fame to shame offers many lessons on how money should not be managed. Making money may look like a tough job. But the toughest job is to manage the money that you made in such a way that it grows and elevates you and the society.

The idea of sharing these two stories is not to scare you, but to caution you. Beware of such pitfalls due to money mismanagement. Let us start educating our kids about money management and make them responsible citizens who care for themselves and for others. The rise and fall of such personalities teach us valuable life lessons.

–X–

Financial Planning

Everything you do in life needs to be planned. Planning helps improve the success rate. If you fail to plan, it means you are planning to fail. Let us see what famous people say about planning.

Stephen Covey, the author of *7 Habits of Successful People*, says: 'Begin with the end in mind.'

Yogi Berra, an American professional baseball player says, 'If you don't know where you are going, you'll end up someplace else.'

Antoine de Saint-Exupéry, an author who has won several of Franc's highest literary awards says: 'A goal without a plan is just a wish.'

Like any other aspect, your finance also needs some planning. To plan your finances, you need to define your financial goals, because that is the base. What are your financial goals?

Let us break this further into two. One is "finance" and another is "goal".

First, please understand that goals are vital for anyone to achieve success. If you do not have a clear direction, then you may be going somewhere away from it. Goals give you direction. Goals show you the path. Goals determine your action.

A financial goal helps you achieve what *you* want to achieve in terms of money. If you don't have a clear set of financial goals, then there are high chances of you slipping out of Zero EMI. You will be firefighting to manage your ad-hoc and huge expenses all through your life.

You may need a lot of money for your kid's education, for their marriage expenses, to buy a new house or a new car, etc. Not everyone needs all of this. Some may not be interested in buying a house. Some may not be interested in buying a car. The needs differ from person to person. What are your needs? Convert them into financial goals. Like any other goal, financial goals must also be SMART—Specific, Measurable, Attainable, Realistic and Time-bound. Else, it will again only be a wish and not an achievement. You may have multiple goals.

Write down the details about all of your goals – How much money do you need? By when do you need this money? Is it five years later, or 10 years later, or 15 years later?

Once you have your goals defined, then the next step is to plan.

The details you wrote down about your goals are the base for your planning exercise. Now, you know how much money you need and by when you need it. Based on this information, keep a monthly target in order to achieve your financial goal.

For example, your kid's marriage is one of your financial goals. You need ₹50 lakhs to meet marriage expenses and you need it exactly 20 years later. Take a stock of what is already in your hand in the form of cash, bank balance, jewels, stocks, investments, etc. Deduct that from the ₹50 lakhs so that you get to know how much more is required in 20 years. If in case you have not saved even a single rupee toward this goal, no worries. You can start now. For ₹50 lakhs required 20 years later to meet your kid's marriage expenses, you need ₹21,000 every month from now to meet this goal (₹50 lakhs divided by 240 months).

Please note that I have not factored inflation while calculating this. The financial advisors will also account for inflation while doing this calculation. However, I am not a financial advisor and hence not considering inflation in order to keep it simple.

By the way it is good to know what inflation is. In simple words, inflation is purchasing power. For example, I can buy 1 liter of petrol with ₹100. Maybe 10 years later I will not be able to buy the same 1 liter of petrol using ₹100. I may get only 0.75 liters or much lesser than that, depending on the petrol price. So, the purchasing power of that ₹100 has come down. This is what we call inflation. The government publishes the inflation rate periodically. It serves as an indicator to know the cost of goods and services. More the inflation, the lesser the purchasing power. Lesser the inflation, the more the purchasing power.

Realistically, the ₹50 lakhs estimated to organize a marriage may not be enough when you want to get married 20 years later. The purchasing power of ₹50 lakhs would have come down. That is why exactly financial advisors' factors inflation also while drafting financial goals. However, let us now forget about inflation and keep it simple. You come up with an estimation or a projection related to each of your financial goals like marriage, a new house, a new car, educational expenses, and much more and then figure out by when you want to achieve these. Find out how much you need to save every month in order to achieve this by so and so date, which will give you clarity toward your goals and help you achieve them as desired.

One more point to note regarding financial planning. If you want to achieve your financial goals, you must get rid of your debts – yes, Zero EMI. Debts can dent your financial goals. Living in debt can be a huge roadblock in your personal finance journey. Before you chart down your financial goals, draw a plan to clear your debts. Debt is a leakage. Having great aspirations and having debt too is like filling water in bucket with hole. You might never be able to fill the bucket. Unfortunately, that is a fact. I want you to genuinely succeed in your life. That will be possible only if you get rid of your debts. Please read the chapters "How to Avoid Loans" and "How to Reduce Loans" to get ideas to kill your debt.

The best thing you can do is say a big NO to the lifestyle-related debts such as buying a new mobile, lavish vacations, etc. Pledge doing this with your own money and not on borrowed money. The best way to meet such lifestyle-related expenses is to add these items as one of your financial goals and then start planning to achieve this. In that way, you can meet these expenses with your own money and not borrow money or get into a debt trap.

Many people make use of the zero percent EMI (no cost EMI) schemes to buy lifestyle-related products such as home appliances, mobile phones and lavish holidays. Please remember that there is no free lunch in business. Even though they say it is no-cost

EMI, there may be hidden costs like processing fees, denied cost reduction, etc. Another important point is that you may end up in a habit to buy things you cannot afford to buy, just because there is a zero percent EMI scheme available. It soon turns into an addiction, and you start buying unaffordable things frequently. Because it is easily available with no cost EMI. You will end up adding more EMIs and landing into a debt trap.

You must be determined not to take loans and live only with cash. And, I think this will be a humongous step toward achieving your financial goals. That is the only way to achieve what you want to achieve.

In a nutshell, define your financial goals, start planning to achieve those goals, say NO to debts and live with Zero EMI. If you follow this, I am sure you will achieve all of your financial goals.

–XI–

Questions in Your Mind

During my keynote speeches, many people asked questions at the end of my speech. That showed their interest towards managing their personal finance. I compiled some of the questions and answers for your reading. Because, I strongly believe it will be useful not only for the people who asked that question but also for the people who have the same question in their mind.

I have surplus cash and also many loans to repay. What should I do with the surplus cash?

Here is my view. When you have many loans, I always suggest paying off high-interest loans first. It reduces interest outflow to a great extent. For example: You have a personal loan, a credit card outstanding, a car loan and a housing loan. The personal loan interest is 14 percent per annum, credit card interest is 48 percent per annum, car loan and housing loan interests are somewhere between 8-10 percent. The costliest debt is the credit card one, so knock it off first so that you save on interest outflow.

Having said that, debt also brings a lot of emotions. It is stressful to deal with many loans and keep track of their due dates. During those stressful times, forget the high-cost loan. Check for your smallest loan and close it, though it is not the costliest one. For example, the personal loan outstanding is ₹5000, the credit card is ₹75,000, the housing loan is ₹15 lakhs and the car loan is ₹35,000. Paying off the smallest debt (personal loan in this case) will give you a sense of achievement and a huge relief. It would also give you the confidence to close off the remaining debts.

Closing the costliest loan is the intelligent way, whereas closing the smallest loan is the psychological way.

You can choose any, depending on your situation.

Will balance transfer affect my CIBIL score?

Let me remind you what balance transfer is. I mentioned it earlier in this book. Balance transfer is nothing but transferring the credit card due amount from one bank to another. There would be a processing fee but no late fee. The new bank will allow you 90 days to repay the dues. It is a tricky situation. Balance transfer results in on-time payment to boost your credit score. Yet, to do balance transfer, you must hold more than one credit card. Whenever you apply for a new credit card to play with balance transfer, it will bring down the average age of all credit accounts. Needless to mention its effect on the credit score. Every time you apply for a credit card, an inquiry is made to the credit report. Each inquiry is potential enough to lower your score. On the other hand, balance transfer helps you save some interest and reduce your debt faster. That is why I said that it is a bit tricky.

Another important factor to be considered while doing balance transfer is the amount you are going to transfer. Ideally, it should not be more than 40-50 percent of your credit card limit. Else, it affects your credit score. The best thing to do is to close the credit card outstanding as credit card debt is the most expensive one.

Why majority of women do not show much interest in finance?

The women workforce in both organized and unorganized sectors deals with money. Still, finance is a scary word and world to most of the women out there.

The fact is that women are more skillful than men in many areas, especially when it comes to finance. Still, finance is a scary word and world to most of the women out there.

Ancient poems and old movie songs indicated that women must be entrusted with money in order to grow your money. Still, finance is a scary word and world to most of the women out there.

In my opinion, many women are dependent on a man from their childhood—maybe her father, her brother, or her husband. This gives them a cushion and keeps them away from monetary transactions. Another reason is that women nowadays are already loaded with a lot of responsibilities at home and at the office. So, when it comes to finance, they tend to outsource it to men in the house.

The fact is: When the women handle finances by themselves, they do a better job than men. Women take informed decisions, whereas men often seem to be impulsive. This characteristic of women helps curtail unnecessary spending.

To build a wealthy, debt-free family, I would request women to take charge of finances. Choose your investments, build assets and most importantly, live debt-free. Trust me, finance is not that scary.

Is gold a good investment?

The disclaimer is that I am not an investment specialist. I specialize in debt management and aim to help my fellow human beings come out of the debt trap and lead a financially independent life. I can share my few cents regarding "gold" as an investment. However, you may want to vet it with your financial advisor.

Gold is certainly a good investment instrument to be in a portfolio, that too if you have exposure to equities/shares. This is because the share market and gold are inversely proportional. When the value of one increases, the other will decrease. So, when you have shares, then better to invest in gold as well. Both will absorb each other's shocks in terms of price fall and will strike a good balance in your portfolio. In a country like India, the demand and the craze around gold will stay despite the advancement in the artificial jewelry segment. Also, I prefer to buy e-gold (Gold ETF) and not the physical gold coins or ornaments. There are various advantages to holding e-gold. You need not worry about its safety or look for a locker to keep it safe. Also, you can liquidate it in the market anytime, that too up to 100 percent of its value in cash and can be repurposed to any other emergency expenses or investments. Though the physical gold offers high liquidity, you cannot liquidate its 100 percent value. If you pledge, you will get 50 percent to 60 percent of the market rate. If you sell, you will lose on the wastage charges. So, it is a smart decision to invest in e-gold if you choose gold as an investment in your portfolio.

Sovereign gold bonds issued by the RBI are also a good option. You can buy this online so that you get a discount of ₹50 per unit/gram. The RBI gives 2 percent to 2.5 percent interest for every holding year. These bonds have a maturity period of eight years and you can come out of it only after the fifth year. Meaning the premature encashment is allowed only after five years. So, if you are looking for a short-term investment of two-three years, sovereign gold bonds may not be a good option.

If I need to buy a home, buying with own fund is advisable instead of taking a loan?

That is ideal. However, the value of the house will be huge. It may not be practically possible for most people to buy a house with their own funds, especially the middle-class, salaried people. If you do not have your own money to buy, then you do not have a choice other than taking a housing loan. As I mentioned earlier in this book, a housing loan is good debt. The value of your house grows over a period. If you take a loan for an item that will grow in value, then it is good debt.

If you buy a house for yourself to live, then there is no discussion about it being a good investment or not. If you are going to buy your second house, then obviously you would not stay there. You would be renting it out. You must select a location wherein the value of the house will grow decently enough. If you buy a house in the areas wherein the prices are already at high and stagnated, there may not be much scope for an increase in value. But, if you buy a house in an upcoming or an underdeveloped area, then there are chances for your house value to increase. You will get a good return on investment. A good research of the area is a must before buying any house. The two important questions you need to ask yourself is: 1) Will the value of the house increase in the future? 2) Will I get a decent rental income from the house?

Irrespective of the purpose of buying a house—to live or to rent it out—if you cannot fund it from your savings, the ideal choice is to take a housing loan.

What is a calculated risk?

You and I take a lot of financial decisions every day without being aware of it. Right from paying your vegetable vendor to buying a new cloth to buying shares—all of them are financial decisions. When you have all the information about the situation or product, then you take an informed decision. When you take an informed decision, you know about the outcome of the decision as well. You know the amount of risk involved, the probability of winning or losing, and you know what returns will come your way. Such a risk is called a calculated risk.

Let us take the example of shares. During the fight against Covid-19, I got a sense of the industries that would boom in the future. The current price of those shares may be less than their worth, due to the share market decline. So, I resolve to do research on the industries such as pharmaceuticals, which will pick up soon after Covid-19. I will do my research about the shares in that industry, will look at the industry's history, judge performance and talk to investment experts for the information on its shares. With all such information well collected, I will choose if I should buy shares or not. If the facts are strongly favoring a company, then I will go ahead and take the risk of investing in their shares. This is an example of calculated risk.

If I have to buy a car, should I have saved money for a very long time?

Yes, you must save money for any high-value item that would reduce in value. This includes high-end mobile phones, cars, electronic gadgets, etc. Taking a loan for these items will hurt you in the long term as it is bad debt. I spoke in detail, in the earlier section of this book, about car loans and its pitfalls. I also narrated what my friend Arjun did to buy his own car.

As this question is specifically about cars, I suggest you add 'buying a car' as one of your financial goals and start working towards it. It is advisable either to enter a mutual fund through Systematic Investment Plan (SIP) or invest strategically elsewhere so that the money also works for you and you reach your goal much faster. Buying a car loan is not advisable at any cost. Remember that buying a car is not an emergency expenditure and it can certainly wait until you have enough money.

Can I convert a personal loan into a mortgage loan/housing loan where ROI is less?

Ans: Personal loan and housing loans are two different products that banks sell. The first one is an unsecured loan and offered based on your income. The bank will obtain your identity documents and verify them. There is no collateral security required to get this loan. Due to this, the interest rate on this loan is slightly higher. On average, the rate is anywhere between 14 percent to 24 percent.

The second one is a secured loan backed by your property. The property will be in the name of the lender and later transferred to your name after you repay the entire dues. That is why it is also called a mortgage loan. As it is a secured loan, the ROI is less when compared to unsecured loans such as personal loans. You cannot transfer or convert your personal loan into a housing loan as the nature of these loans is quite different from each other. You need to repay them separately.

What is the difference between balance transfer and restructure?

When you transfer the entire outstanding amount from one credit card to another credit card, it is called balance transfer. When you work with your bank to alter the repayment schedule, it is called "restructuring".

Once you have done the balance transfer, then the entire outstanding amount is to be paid before or on the completion of 90 days for the new credit card. You will not be charged any interest, however there will be a processing fee. The fees differ from bank to bank. You can also transfer the balance at the end of 90 days back to the original credit card or to your entirely new credit card. In one of the previous questions, I answered about how balance transfer can affect your CIBIL score. So, please be cautious while doing so.

On restructuring, the entire outstanding amount will be converted into manageable, repayable chunks with the consent of both the banker and the debtor. It gives relief to the debtor as the restructuring provides an extension of tenure with reduced EMI and at times an interest waiver as well. The restructured schedule must be honored promptly in order to rebuild your CIBIL score. On a case-to-case basis, the bank may approve or reject the proposal to restructure.

When buying a land worth 20 lakhs, whether to buy with my own funds or use 50 percent of my money and take a loan for five

years (where I can invest the remaining 50 percent of my own funds in gold/bonds for five years)? Which is better?

My choice will be to buy the land with my own funds. If you are going to take a loan for five years, I think you are talking about a personal loan. If yes, then the interest rate will be anywhere between 14 to 24 percent per annum. Are you sure about getting more returns than the rate of interest you would be paying? Will the returns be more than 14 percent? Have you done enough research before choosing the investment instrument? Only the stock market can give such returns. What is your risk absorbing capacity? Please try to answer these questions before making the decision of investing the cash in hand and buying a loan to purchase the land. Having said that, being debt-free and investing your own money in hand is the ideal way.

Is it better to invest in mutual funds or shares?

Again, the disclaimer is that I am not an investment specialist. I specialize in debt management. Coming to your question, it is a vague, open-ended question and the answers to it are many. My two cents are: Mutual fund houses invest in equity and in debt market so that the risk is balanced to some extent. Investing in the share market needs sound knowledge backed by solid research as market conditions are not in our control. The volatility and the risk involved are high as compared to mutual funds. You need to talk to your family or your financial advisor to choose the instrument that best suits your financial goals.

Mutual funds, shares, SIP, LIC, PPF – Which is the best?

Ans: All of them are different products and come with their own pros and cons. One must consider their own product knowledge, risk appetite, personal situations, cash flow and financial goals before investing. All I can say is that please do not put all your eggs in one basket. Have as much diversification as possible, which will help you strike a balance when there is a price fall in the product's value.

How good mutual funds are as compared to other investments like NPS, government bonds, etc.?

Ans: Again, all of them are different products and come with their own pros and cons. Mutual funds give a number of choices with 45+ fund houses for investors to choose from. SIP allows to handle market fluctuations and price shocks.

NPS investments have the lowest charges among investment products. We need to consider the cost of investment as well. They too invest in government bonds, corporate debt, equity, etc. NPS investments up to ₹50,000 are tax exempted under 80CCD (1B)[1]. This is over and above the 1.5 lakh deduction available under 80C[2]. If you are in the topmost tax bracket (30 percent), then you straight away save ₹15,000.

Government bonds come with low risk, which means they will give low returns. Every investment comes with risks and returns. Again, risks and returns are inversely proportional. More the risk, the higher the returns. Lesser the risk, the lower the returns. You

---

[1] **Section 80CCD(1B)** of the Income Tax Act of India is a new sub-section, which offers an additional deduction of up to Rs. 50,000/-for contributions made by individual taxpayers towards the NPS.

[2] **Section 80C** of the Income Tax Act of India is a clause that points to various expenditures and investments that are exempted from Income Tax. It allows for a maximum deduction of up to Rs.1.5 lakh every year from an investor's total taxable income.

need to consider your financial goals and risk absorbing capacity before deciding to choose an instrument.

Will any private bank accept for restructuring?

Yes, all banks accept restructuring. However, on a case-to-case basis, the bank may approve or reject the restructure proposal because restructuring is not a profitable solution for banks. The only advantage for them is that they can recover the principal amount, which otherwise would have been written off. The applicant must put all their efforts into talking to the bank's branch, the head office, and the Banking Ombudsman. Banking Ombudsman is the judicial authority and they help resolve customer complaints related to banking services and products. However, the Banking Ombudsman should be the last resort after your attempts with the chosen bank are not successful.

What is the difference between health insurance and medical insurance?

Medical Insurance, or Mediclaim, provides coverage for your hospitalization expenses. Whereas health insurance gives you a comprehensive coverage. It not only covers hospitalization expenses but also post-hospitalization charges, ambulance costs and compensation for lost income.

Mediclaim covers hospitalization costs toward accidents and other pre-illness, meaning it is applicable only when you have a pre-existing disease at the time of purchasing the insurance policy. A cashless facility is available under the Mediclaim plan. For hospitals that do not offer a cashless facility, you can pay out of your pocket and later have the expenses reimbursed by the insurer. You need to preserve all hospital-related documents of your case, such as prescription, medical bills, discharge summary, etc. These policies can be taken for both an individual and a family.

Comprehensive health insurance policy comes with various features such as pre- and post-hospitalization coverage for 30 to 60 days, ambulance charges, no claim bonus (like with car insurance), free medical checkups and of course tax benefits. You can claim ₹25,000 under Section 80D[3] and ₹30,000 if you are a senior citizen.

The terms and conditions of each insurance provider may differ. So, please read the terms, conditions, features before buying an insurance policy.

My company provides me health insurance. Do I need to buy additional policies on my own?

Ans: A strong YES is the answer. Your company may provide your health insurance, but you are covered as long as you are employed with that company. The moment you step out of the company, you lose the benefit. Many people do not realize this fact and at times stay without any cover until another employment opportunity. In case of any unfortunate incident during this period of unemployment, they shell out huge money from their savings or end up taking loans to meet the medical expenses.

It happened to one of my friends who was laid off from the company all of a sudden. He was looking for another job. Unfortunately, he met with an accident soon after and was hospitalized. The doctors advised surgery in his right leg. The surgery cost plus the hospital expenses came around ₹2.25 lakhs.

---

[3] Section 80D of the Income Tax Act offers tax benefits for the medical insurance premium paid. This is in addition to Section 80C tax breaks of up to Rs 1.5 lakh.

When the hospital asked if he had any insurance, he realized and missed having health insurance. The only coverage he had was what the last company provided. It was a huge slap on his face, but he luckily had some savings and could pay the hospital bills. If in case he did not have enough savings, he would have taken a loan to meet the surgery expenses.

Even during the time of your employment, you do not have control over the insurance policy, its coverage, etc. Your company only controls the insurance policy it provides, and it can decrease the coverage amount, alter the terms and conditions and modify the per person ceiling (if in case your dependents are also covered). You do not have control over the policy there.

Secondly, in a normal scenario, you come out of employment at old age. If you buy a new policy at an older age, the premium amount will be higher. Many are unaware of this fact and burn their fingers when they buy a new policy at an older age. Remember to enter an insurance policy early at your age to enjoy low premium benefits.

The medical treatments are expensive, and diseases do not check whether you got money or not before hitting you. Nowadays, lifestyle-related diseases have become common and treatment expenses are huge. To meet such medical expenses, you must have a health insurance policy with you.

Conclusion

Congratulations on reaching here. It shows your keenness to improve your personal finance and come out of debt.

Many of us are tied… to our financial commitments. Tied to our EMIs. Zero EMI must be the target of everyone. From 0 percent EMI to Zero EMI, the transformation requires a lot of effort from your side. It needs a lot of financial discipline. Believe me, it is a worthwhile effort.

If you are longing for financial freedom, you must have Zero EMI. People say that with a lot of wealth comes financial freedom. In my view, you must first stop the leakage. When there is a hole in the bucket, how much ever you pour, it is going to leak. Maybe you will never be able to fill it. Debt and EMIs are leakages you must cover up to grow wealth and attain financial freedom. EMIs do not take holidays; however, you see your assets taking holidays. That is why I say everyone must have Zero EMI. Debt is Dangerous. Debts attract interest. Interest never sleeps.

To attain financial freedom, you must avoid taking loans and reduce your existing loans, so that you have Zero EMI and you can lead a stress-free life, financially. Control your finances rather than be controlled by them. *Your financial wellness is the key to a good life.* Develop good money habits like tracking your expenses, not using credit cards, staying away from loans, building emergency funds, etc. Plan your finances well. Start having financial goals.

Money management is an art. Start teaching your kids about money management. Most of the families do not do that. It is our duty to make the next generation financially literate. It is one of the important life skills we need to equip our children with. More than assets, we need to impart to our children the knowledge and experience we have.

This book is a response to my childhood struggles. The most horrible thing in life is poverty during childhood,' I say, having experienced so myself.

All that I want my fellow human beings to do is "avoid loans", lead a Zero EMI life and give your children the most pleasant childhood. My heartfelt thanks to you for reading this book.

www.ingramcontent.com/pod-product-compliance
Lightning Source LLC
Chambersburg PA
CBHW021446210526
45463CB00002B/657